DANIEL
SEVEN

The Beginning and the Ending of
All Times As We Know It

DANIEL SEVEN

The Beginning and the Ending of All Times As We Know It

In the beginning God created the heavens and the earth. And the earth was without form, and void, and darkness was upon the face of the deep. And the Spirit of God moved upon the face of the deep. And God said, Let there be light and there was light. And God saw the light that it was good: and God divided the light from darkness. And God called the light Day, and the darkness he called Night. And evening and the morning were the first day. Genesis 1:1-5

And the Spirit and the bride say, Come. And let him heareth say, Come. And let him that is athirst come. And whosoever will, let him take of the water of life freely.

Shedrick Crosby

ARPress
45 Dan Road Suite 5
Canton, MA 02021

Hotline: 1(888) 821-0229
Fax: 1(508) 545-7580

Ordering Information:
Quantity sales. Special discounts are available on quantity purchases by corporations, associations, and others. For details, contact the publisher at the address above.

Printed in the United States of America.

ISBN-13:   Softcover   979-8-89330-341-4
             eBook   979-8-89330-343-8
             Hardback   979-8-89330-344-5

Library of Congress Control Number: 2024900498

TABLE OF CONTENTS

The Beginning 1

God Created "Times and Laws" 4

Daniel 7 5

An earthly Imitation 11

How Our Calendar Came To Be 19

The Mark of the Beast: "666" 22

Now Let's Look at the Months 24

The "Laws" of Rome 26

Christmas or Christ Mass 30

Have You Been Deceived? 32

Christmas Tree 34

Christmas 36

Adding to the Word of God 38

The Televangelists 41

Did You Know? 46

Study the Old Testament for Examples 48

"As an African" 52

Destiny 54

The Pope 57

The Influence of Rome upon the World Today 64

Your Destiny 68

Seven Mountains... 69

The Fourth Beast's "Laws" 71

Ethiopian Eunuch Saved by Doing What?..................... 84

The Church.. 88

The Ten Plagues of Egypt 102

The Exodus 104

Judas Commits Suicide.................................... 107

About the Author.. 166

In loving memories to my parents Julius and Mildred Floyd Crosby and my two sisters Julius Ann Crosby and Brenda Sue Crosby Cobb

Shedrick Crosby's Website and Trailers

Author's Website:
DanielSevenbyShedrickCrosby.Com

Daniel Seven Book Trailer:
https://www.youtube.com/watch?v=6BzCJ55lExI

Author's Summary of Life Trailer:
**https://www.dropbox.com/s/rob0c0we82cwlr6/Crosby%20BVT.
mp4?dl=0**

"THE FIRST BEAST"

MEDES

800's-500 BC

THE LION

"THE SECOND BEAST"
PERSIA
550-300 BC

THE BEAR

"THE THIRD BEAST"

GREECE

700-480 BC

THE LEOPARD

"THE FOURTH BEAST"

753-PRESENT

THE IORN TEETH

And he shall speak great words against the most High, and shall wear out the saints of the most High, and think to change times and laws: and they shall be given into his hand until a time and times and the dividing of time. (Daniel 7:25)

I was born in 1958 in Pensacola, Florida. I grew up in a neighborhood called Shanty Town—yeah, Shanty Town—and close by was another neighborhood called Hawkshaw and another called the Tan Yard. We also have Ebonwood. But I don't think we can beat Porkenbeans in Miami.

Talking about self-esteem, right out of the gates of life: "Where are you from?" "Uh, Shanty Town"— and not Malibu or Staten Island.

Now some of these neighborhoods that were predominately black have been displaced or bought out, and townhouses and condo-like homes have replaced them. The main reason is that these areas were in the downtown area where they have built the Civic Center and close to the beach area or by the downtown   water area.

Some years ago, they changed Shanty Town to Englewood Heights, but you got the same houses from the 1960s still there. Only the name has changed.

It was a neighborhood not without family problems, but we did care about one another. If I did wrong, my parents were told, and I would get punished, or the neighbor would punish me and tell my parents why. There was a time when my parents weren't home, and my neighbors kept me until they came home.

Little did some know black and white kids were already playing together during segregation. Then when desegregation happened, you simply had more black and white kids playing together.

In the late sixties after desegregation, my sixth-grade teacher was a beautiful white teacher, and we were her first class. I was her first "citizen of the week" recipient. On many occasions she would come to

Shanty Town where I lived and would take me to her nice home to play with her son and her husband, who was a Navy pilot here in Pensacola. Mind you, I was the only Black at these events, which would become commonplace for me. This situation took two families to pull this off, mine and hers, during the Civil Rights Movement.

Growing up was tough because about 90 percent of my clothes came from the thrift stores. I got new clothes at the beginning of school and maybe during the summer. I went barefoot for many days and without socks. I can remember a time when I stepped on a nail, and it went into the heel of my foot. My parents couldn't afford a doctor, and the hospital was a few blocks away. Many Blacks couldn't afford hospital or doctor visits, and many didn't trust them either. Really the only time I saw a doctor was to get shots for school and pills for worms because we played in the dirt a lot.

As a child I was taught the Bible by my dad, and there was a time early in the morning I went to sit on the porch alone. I asked the Lord, "Why did you make me?" I couldn't have been more than ten years of age. Why would I be thinking of that? I mean, go outside and shoot some marbles or spin some tops, or how about toss some horseshoes because who cares who made you? I do. The devil was after me at a young age too because I stole and lied. I had found a .22-caliber bullet on the ground in the driveway.

One morning when everyone was asleep, I ventured out to the front steps which were made of concrete. I hit that bullet as hard as I could, and there was a loud bang. I was shaken and turned around to see where the bullet had gone. There were houses all around in the neighborhood, but no one came outside. I simply say now, "Oh my God"; how foolish that was. The bullet could have hit me or some neighbor. Maybe you have similar stories in your life.

Now back to my story about the bullet. To pull this off, shooting the bullet, I had to hide the bullet and sneak out of the house. This brings to mind this scripture of two people who hid themselves.

Now the serpent was more subtil than any beast of the field which the LORD God had made. And he said unto the woman, "Yea, hath God said, Ye shall not eat of every tree of the garden?" And the woman said unto the serpent, "We may eat of the fruit of the trees of the garden: but of the fruit of the tree, which is in the midst of the garden, God hath said, Ye shall not eat of it, neither shall ye touch it, lest ye die."

And the serpent said unto the woman, "Ye shall not surely die. [The serpent changed one word to corrupt the word of God to deceive Eve, the single word not.] For God doth know that in the day ye eat thereof, then your eyes shall be opened, and ye shall be as gods, knowing good and evil." [This was the truth, so to deceive someone, you need a little bit of truth and a little bit of a lie.] And when the woman saw that the tree was good for food, and that it was pleasant to the eyes, and a tree to be desired to make one wise, she took of the fruit thereof, and did eat, and gave also unto her husband with her; and he did eat. And the eyes of them both were opened, and they knew that they were naked; and they sewed fig leaves together and made themselves aprons. And they heard the voice of the LORD God walking in the garden in the cool of the day: and Adam and his wife hid themselves from the presence of the LORD God amongst the trees of the garden. (Genesis 3:1–8)

(They hid from God the way I hid that bullet.) Why? Because it was wrong? Sometimes it's okay to hide things to protect them for some reason—but not in a malicious way. If you are prudent about your life, you will learn that you develop character traits. Some are good, and some are bad.

I also remember a time and it was a few that my mom took me to a major clothing store in the neighborhood for shopping. As soon as we entered the doors, we could see white kids playing with toys and riding tricycles, but my mom wouldn't let us touch anything and said we were being watched every move we made.

My mom would say, "Don't touch that." So how does that affect little kids? I stole as a little kid, but my parents didn't know that, so I thought it was because they didn't teach me to steal. One day my mom said, "Where did you get that from?" and I made up a lie. It was somewhat similar to when God asked Adam and Eve, "Who told you that you were naked? Have you eaten from the tree I told you not to eat from?" So, Adam and Eve started passing the buck by telling on each other. My mom knew that I didn't have any money. Now I'm a thief and a liar, all because I saw someone have something that I couldn't have or touch through temptations. My childhood growing up was similar to the other kids because we played sports and games in the dirt. I remember one game called "Eat the Peg" where you had tries in the dirt making a knife do certain things, and if not and you lost, the winner would push a peg or a little stick in the ground, and you would have to pick it out of the dirt with your mouth. As mentioned earlier about the times we went to the doctors at the health department to get shots and pills for worms because we played in the dirt.

In elementary school I was a part of school plays and a good dancer. I had an uncle, my father's only brother, who would come by the house and would ask me to dance and do the splits, and boy, I would shuffle those feet and do those splits, and he would give me a quarter.

One day as I was getting off the bus, my daddy's car was home early from work (because he did the 7–3 p.m. shift). Once inside, I saw him and my mom hurriedly getting dressed. They were getting ready to go to view my uncle's body; he had been stabbed to death.

I was told some years later what had happened. My uncle was messing around with someone's girlfriend while he was in prison, and the man told my uncle to stop, or he would kill him. So, the man got out of prison and found out where my uncle lived and drew him across the street and cut him up. My uncle tried to run, but the man sliced his leg, and as my dad told the story, he could put his fist in his brother's back due to how big the hole was from the stabbings. I remember the funeral reception, and I walked across the street to see where my uncle tried to run and was killed. His bloody handprints stayed on the wall of this white house for many years. The devil got three people that day: the killer, my uncle for sure because he can't come back and repent, and the girlfriend.

In 1970, due to domestic violence my dad went to work one morning and came back in the evening to an empty house. My mom took the four youngest kids to San Diego at Imperial Beach, California, to the Del Sol Apartments. The three oldest kids would come to California later. I come from a large family, having three sisters and three brothers. My dad was a Korean War veteran and dealt with racism on his job plus the loss of his brother. I guess he couldn't take his frustrations out on anyone else, so he took them out on us. My mom didn't know where she was going; that was just where we ended up, some two thousand miles away.

I attended Montgomery Junior High and there a Mexican teacher became a father figure to me. I spent many days and nights at his home, and he took me to worship, to the World's Fair, and to a USC Trojans game. This was at a time when the USC Trojans would come out of the horse at halftime. During the weekends I was in the metal shop with him, and he made me foreman. He taught me many things that I use to this very day.

In my third year at Montgomery Junior High, they took some of the smartest kids, including me, to make a film at the world's largest zoo, the San Diego Zoo. The film was to be shown around the world at that time, but I never got to see it because the day of the showing we were headed back to Florida on a Greyhound bus. My mom and dad had gotten back together, only to divorce some thirty years later.

So, I'm kind of well-rounded in race, and in my years, I have been in mixed relationships. California was nothing like the South because Mexicans date blacks and whites, and whites date blacks and Mexicans. Wow. Of course, we would have our fights here and there and walkouts from school. At times there were racial fights, and I tried to steer clear because I wanted to get my education. I was an A-B Honor Roll student.

I can remember when I first got to the apartments, I was trying to find friends. I got with a group of boys, and one night they wanted to go to a main store called White Front. I had no money at all and was just going for the ride, trying to make friends. Once at the store, they all separated and said, "we'd all meet back by the entrance." Beside the car they all started pulling out different cans of spray paint and airplane glue. This was a time of uppers and downers, LSD, opium, heroin, cocaine, tranquilizers, and pot. I stole as a little boy, but at this time of my life stealing wasn't a part of it. I couldn't wait to get back home and never did that again.

I was puzzled at times when walking to school because I would see socks balled up on the ground; I thought someone had lost their socks. Now, if you could remember I grew up at times without shoes and socks. So, I'm thinking, someone is losing their socks.

So, one day I was so curious that I picked one up and opened the sock. Copper paint had been sprayed on the sock, and at other times there would be silver paint too. These kids were getting high to and from school by sniffing paint, and you could tell who was doing it because their lips would have copper or silver on them. There was word in the neighborhood that one of the kids who had sniffed a lot of paint got a hole in his brain.

There was a time when my mom had bought me a red Honda Trail 70 to ride in the canyons because I was a good kid by obeying her and keeping my grades up, and it was my birthday. So, I began to befriend some white kids in the area and pulled up at the community laundromat, and some of the black kids were jealous. They started picking at how I spoke, like from the country. Coming from Florida, I didn't say "you guys" because I usually said "y'all" instead. Then one of the big guys (see, they taught me well) came over and kicked my motorcycle. In seconds I jumped off my bike and picked him up, and I aimed for the corner edge of the big green dumpster and rammed him into it. From that day forward he was my friend.

I had to fight to have friends then. Who needs friends? What if the kid had a knife or gun? Think about this now: jealousy is as old as the beginning of time. Remember in Genesis, the third chapter, how God told Adam and Eve, "In the day you eat thereof you shall surely die"? Now Adam and Eve didn't know what death was, so the devil deceived the serpent because he was so wise (pride), and the serpent deceived Eve to betray God and to go against God's word, meaning to disobey.

So, in the process of time, Adam and Eve had two sons, one named Cain and the other named Abel. And Cain killed Abel because Abel offered up a better sacrifice, and this was due to jealousy. So, the devil was everywhere in black people and in white people and in old people and in young people. I didn't know him as prevalent around my life and in my life as I do today at the age of sixty-two and he still gets me even now. You know he's been at this a lot longer than I will ever live.

I never got the chance to say goodbye to my teacher so many years later I called him to tell him what an influence he had been in my life, but he couldn't remember me, because I believe dementia had set in. I also sought to find my sixth-grade teacher to thank her but never could find her. Then in about 2019 I was told by someone who knew her that she had passed. I can remember once my daddy and mom got back together in 1973, and my dad wanted to make up to us and he bought some property and a brand-new trailer. I was a hard worker and an A-B Honor Roll student, and one day he said "Shad?" and I said, "Yes, sir?" "Come and take me to the bank." I was just learning to drive, and I was thinking that he was going to deposit some money.

Once at the bank and before the teller he said, "do you have a dollar?" I said, "yes sir", and gave him the dollar. He then turned and gave me the title to his 1968 Plymouth Fury. That meant a lot to him and me. I'm crying as I write this at the age of sixty-two. In 2009 my dad, whom I love to this day, drove to Pensacola from Tallahassee. He had dementia at the time, but we didn't know it. He came to ask my mom for forgiveness for how he had treated her. His wife at the time didn't tell us about his condition because they were having marital problems and she didn't really like us.

One weekend we traveled to see our dad. We had told his wife what time we would be there, and it's about a three-hour drive. When we got there, no one was home. We were ringing the doorbell and knocking, and no answer. We walked the streets to see neighbors, and some commented on the marriage, and it wasn't good.

Well, we came back and sat on the porch, and in about an hour or two she pulled up, and Daddy wasn't with her. She got out with a pretended smile, hoping that we had left, and opened the door to the house. As we entered, there came our dad out of the bedroom. All that time he was there, struggling with dementia.

Think. My daddy understood that there was something going on with his mind called dementia. He knew the word of God and needing to ask for forgiveness from my mom. So, he drove a six hour round trip to Pensacola to ask for forgiveness, because he knew that once his mind got too far gone, he couldn't get forgiveness from God, because you have to ask for it. Now think about that. How many people have lived and have died with dementia and couldn't correct the sins of their lives?

Soon after that, his wife put him in a nursing home and didn't tell us where—and due to HIPAA, no one told us. At that time, he didn't know that his oldest daughter was going through chemo in 2012 for lymphoma, and in three months of chemo she caught an infection and was pronounced brain-dead. We never saw her doctor to tell us how this could be, and that hospital was so nasty to us.

A week into this the head doctor of the ICU wanted the family to pull the plug, but the family said no because we want to know what happened here. The doctor was beside himself and said with a loud voice, "If this was my mom, I wouldn't hesitate to pull the plug." But of course, it wasn't his mom. Then he said, "God already made his decision," but God didn't give her chemo. Then he said, "Next year, in 2014, you won't have this decision"—as if to say, "We will pull the plug without your consent." My mom was crying.

I said to the two social workers, basically, "Get this man away from my sister Judy, and move her to another floor, and find her a place to go." They found her a nursing home in Georgia.

Three months after that my next oldest sister, Brenda, died from a heart attack in her sleep. Although she was sickly, I believe this came from seeing her sister on life support, and she knew the outcome wasn't good because Brenda Sue was an LPN. So, my mom lost two daughters in three months, and this was devastating to our family.

I visited my sister every month for five years, at times with my mom and other family members. During a visit two years into my sister's stay, we asked the nursing staff, "What about her cancer?" They said they weren't treating her for cancer. Well, of course not; we just want to see what they would say. So, we wanted to speak to the doctor, but he wasn't there.

I had him to call me. About a month later he calls, and his regular spiel is "Ah, she has a fever due to the infection, and her blood pressure is so-and-so." I said, "What about the cancer," and he stumbled and began to say her lipids were thus-and-such, and I said, "You know she's there because she has cancer," and he said that he would get back to me. That was about 2015, and it is now 2021. He never called back. At that time, she received a new doctor.

My dad died in 2014 from dementia in Tallahassee, and we weren't invited and didn't know where he was buried until 2020. There is a law in Florida against elder abuse, and we didn't know at the time because his present wife kept us from visiting our father.

My sister on life support died in 2018. My beautiful mom toughed it out but couldn't overcome that her two oldest daughters had died before she did, so she had three strokes and died in 2019. At that time the funeral homes became commonplace for us, and at my mom's funeral I asked the Lord to give us a break.

"But of the tree of the knowledge of good and evil, thou shalt not eat of it: for in the day that thou eatest thereof thou shalt surely die" (Genesis 2:17).

Also, at a young age I liked army movies and was amazed at how they fought and marched. I was you could say intrigued or amazed by them but not wanting to be like them, or so I thought. I was an A-B Honor Roll student from the first grade to the twelfth grade, and I graduated with honors. I had an academic scholarship to Talladega University but went into the Marines instead. The pay wasn't great in the 1970s, but one of the things I did was to give my mom an allotment for forty-five dollars every month for four and a half years. She used to tell me that she loved to go to the mailbox and get her check. I also made her my beneficiary for twenty thousand dollars if I was killed while in the military. I know that's not enough money in exchange for a life.

I served my country as a Marine from 1976 to 1980. I swore to defend this country from enemies foreign and domestic. My swearing-in was presided over by Governor George Wallace as they wheeled him out at Montgomery AFEEC—and what a sight that was, knowing his history. He was humbling.

I was at first a mortar man and then after pains in my back from a beach landing exercise in 1976 I was able to change jobs (MOS) in 1978 to an embassy guard from 1978 to 1980.

Military life was very organized and disciplined but also sinful. In Jacksonville, North Carolina—or Jville, as most Marines called it—I was stationed at Camp Geiger down the road from Camp Lejeune. Night life was wild and crazy because in Jville you had this one street that was a block long, and when you got to the railroad, you were out of the town. Most Marines went to this part of town when they got paid, and you would have salespeople standing in front of their stores yelling and hollering at you to come into their store saying to buy this boom box or this suit or how about these shoes.

Then there's the strip clubs and the X-rated movies, and you were broke when you got back to base. Other than playing war games, that was the life of a Marine. Some of those things affected me even later in life when finding my God and even after finding my God.

I had the privilege to see Ambassador Andrew Young, the first black ambassador to the UN, twice when he came to the American embassy in Lagos, Nigeria. Then at my second post in 1979 at the embassy in Bonn, Germany, I guarded Secretary of State Cyrus Vance in a beautiful castle. He came there to get help with the takeover of the American embassy in Iran.

During my short stay in the military, I was one of "the Few, the Proud, the Marines." I ranked quickly, and while in boot camp at Parris Island, out of approximately eighty Marines I was number ten. I was promoted to PFC out of boot camp "meritoriously."

Once getting to Camp Geiger, which is a part of Camp Lejeune, in an infantry unit as a mortar man I became the number-one A-gunner of all of Camp Lejeune, Camp Johnson, and Camp Geiger for winning the 60mm mortar competition. I was promoted to Corporal, again meritoriously. See Leatherneck magazine write-up; see "Meritorious Mass."

I could have been a Sergeant in less than two years in the Marines, but I ran into a wall called racism and discrimination.

Thou shalt not avenge, nor bear any grudge against the children of thy people, but thou shalt love thy neighbour as thyself: I am the Lord. (Leviticus 19:18)

And as ye would that men should do to you, do ye also to them likewise. (Luke 6:31)

Let me explain. Really, the CEO of Echo Company wasn't promoting many blacks to Sergeant anyway because the black sharp corporals who trained me were busted down to privates because they got angry at constantly being passed over for promotion. Then I came to outrank them. In fact, just recently, in 2021, a black Marine colonel who was passed over three times will now be a brigadier general.

During this time, I was having back pains from an amphibious beach landing and all of the exercising training (three- and five-mile forced marches) with all of that equipment (pack and mortar) on my back. Yes, we carried the mortars on our backs; no jeeps to carry them because a 60mm mortar is considered a lightweight field artillery weapon.

Now after I won the 60mm competition in late 1977 or early '78, the battalion did a "wife swap" by sending my CEO and staff of Echo Company to Fox Company, and Fox Company's CEO and staff came to Echo Company. Fox Company was discriminating. They knew I'd won this competition and had a write-up in Leatherneck magazine, and now I was over the mortar squad. I was promoted to Corporal in a Meritorious Mass before a battalion, which is all of the Company watching me get these awards. The new CEO sent me to the fields and sent another Corporal to the Promotion Board who I was senior to. My men came to me and said, "Corporal Crosby, you should have gone to the Promotion Board." I had been with them for eighteen months.

The other Corporal was new to the unit and didn't know anything about the mortars or how to run a unit. So, when I got back from the fields, this corporal was a sergeant over me. To add insult to injury, battalion now wanted to see this "great mortar section" in operation, not knowing that I was the only one chosen to compete from my squad and company.

I was with all of the top brass on a mountain while now the newly appointed sergeant was down in the valley with the mortar squad. I called the "live fire" as a corporal (which is a sergeant's position). The CEOs and staff praised me for a job well done.

Getting That Pack Off My Back

I started going to Jacksonville Community College at night while not in the fields to become an officer. Get this: I was paying my own way, and at this time in the '70s, we didn't make a lot of money. I did this because I had to get that pack off my back. I had decided to become an officer or go to embassy duty.

I was called to the captain's office. On my way there, I passed my picture on the wall titled "Marine of the Month." Also on the wall was this big faded American flag that no one wanted to paint but me and I did a good job.

The captain said, "Corporal Crosby, you won't be able to go to school anymore."

I said, "Why not, sir?"

And he said, "Because you were trained to fight."

In seconds running through my mind at the age of eighteen, I said, "How did you get to where you're at"?

"Left, right, 'Aye aye, sir.'"

I went across the hall to the first sergeant, who hadn't been transferred, and he knew what I had done for the unit. I asked, "Can I go to embassy duty?"

He said, "Get your paperwork ready," and after eighteen months I was gone.

Once I got to Africa, at the American embassy in Lagos, Nigeria, we were short a Marine who was sick with malaria, and we had three places to guard: a new embassy on Ikoy Island, the old embassy, and an annex. Gunny said, "If you stand duty for a month straight, I will give you more days off," and he did.

While standing duty I began to shift my feet and try standing on different floor mats. Over time I bought new shoes due to lower back pains. I eventually went to the embassy doctor, and they sent me to a local doctor, and he performed an IVP by shooting dye into me.

I was called to the embassy to see the doctor and the nurse. He began to ask me all types of questions about my health and parents, and I said, "What is this about?"

He said, "The dye showed only one kidney on your right side." This was the side I was having all of my back pains. I was sent to Frankfurt, Germany, to Walter Reed Hospital to see if this was true, and it was. I was born with only one kidney, and there's only a 1 percent chance of that. My parents of course were worried.

No one said I was to be discharged but finding out just recently that I'd been born without a vital organ, the protocol was to be discharged. So off I went to my next duty station to Bonn, Germany, with this continued right flank and low back pain. I complained the whole year in Bonn, and after Bonn, I was honorably discharged in 1980.

So, I fought with the VA for over forty years for disability on my back condition and was just awarded disability in 2021. I've had two back surgeries, and the VA only went back three years for back pay. That's what you get for being all you can be for your country.

In 1981 some time had passed, and my wife was pregnant with our first child. I got a knock on the door one early morning, and it was two young men, a black and a white, wanting to talk to me about the

Lord—and no, they weren't Jehovah's Witnesses. I was attentive to their conversation and learned a lot that I have been sharing with you.

And he shall speak great words against the most High, and shall wear out the saints of the most High, and think to change times and laws: and they shall be given into his hand until a time and times and the dividing of time. (Daniel 7:25)

THE BEGINNING

"In the beginning God created the heaven and the earth" (Genesis 1:1). Not man, because he has no power to change God's laws, and man wasn't created by himself; someone had to make him too.

And the earth was without form, and void; and darkness was upon the face of the deep. And the Spirit of God moved upon the face of the waters. And God said, "let there be light": and there was light. And God saw the light, that it was good: and God divided the light from the darkness. And God called the light Day, and the darkness he called Night. And the evening and the morning were the first day. (Genesis 1:2–5)

Everyone should have a plan when they are creating something and a strategy for the future, because things don't always go as planned. One may have a Plan a or Plan B and maybe even a Plan C; now that's God. As builders ourselves—because we come from this God—we like our houses to have this type of kitchen or master bedroom or our cars to have this many seats and horsepower and what type of family will we have?

You know that when you are building, the contractor might cut corners here, and you might spend more money there, and at other times "all hell breaks loose." I know because I've had a house built before. That's what happened to my God. From raising a family, I know

1

how that feels when all hell breaks loose; likewise, when being raised in a family of 9 and having and wife and four children of my own. I think I might qualify as an expert in that field.

In the beginning the Almighty God took something from nothing and he "began" to create. This term, *beginning,* is key to all that is about the Lord because there has to be an ending. How will it end?

So, *time* starts right then. The clock is ticking.

The world was without form, but someone made it round. It was void, and darkness was upon the face of the deep. The world was full of water. Then because it was dark, He created light, and He called the light Day, and the dark he called Night, and the evening and the morning were the *first day.*

Hold it right there. The whole world misses this part of the creation—that the evening and morning were the first day. God continued to teach us how He created time in Genesis for seven days, and it was good, and the evening and the morning formed each day. God is creating His calendar for the creation of man and not vice versa. The Lord never mentions the term midnight, or that twelve a.m. starts another day. So, who changed it? The Fourth Beast. According to Jewish belief, the new day begins at sunset, which gives us "evening and then morning" when the sun rises as the shape of a day.

Everything that God is, the Beast isn't, so we have "God = good" and "evil = devil." There will always be *opposition to the truth.* "Yea, let God be true, but every man a liar; as it is written, that thou mightest be justified in thy sayings, and mightest overcome when thou art judged" (Romans 3:4).

In the 2020s, how shall we escape the punishment of God? Because for good reasons or bad reasons, we know the truth today. We aren't in the caveman days like the Jews or Pilate, who said, "Art thou a king then?" Jesus answered, "Thou sayest that I am a king. To this end was

I born, and for this cause came I into the world, that I should bear witness unto the truth. Every one that is of the truth heareth my voice" (John 18:37). The word of God is truth.

"Pilate saith unto him, what is truth? And when he had said this, he went out again unto the Jews, and saith unto them, I find in him no fault at all" (vs. 38). This was a governor who didn't know what an insurrection is, who was a racist, who didn't know what truth is but will tell a lie instead, and who will kill an innocent man who committed no crime and let a robber go free. This governor has the Mark of the Beast "666" (which is a way of believing in this life).

"He shall speak great words against the most High, and shall wear out the saints of the most High". (Daniel 7:25).

"But ye have a custom, that I should release unto you one at the Passover: will ye therefore that I release unto you the King of the Jews?" Then cried they all again, saying, "Not this man, but Barabbas." Now Barabbas was a robber. (John 18:39–40)

Two people I wouldn't want to be when Jesus comes back, and that is a Roman and a Jew because they crucified my Lord.

GOD CREATED "TIMES AND LAWS"

Remember, the Almighty God created time and not we ourselves. And at first (no pun intended), He called every day by a number, and He didn't give them names like Sunday, Monday, Tuesday, Wednesday, Thursday, Friday, and Saturday—to say nothing of the months: January, February, March, April, May, June, July, August, September, October, November, and December. And what about the holidays like Easter, Christmas, Saint Patrick's Day, Saint Valentine's Day, Thanksgiving Day, Halloween, Father's and Mother's Day? These inventions were created by the "Fourth Beast." (Do your due diligence and study and Google these events and how they started.)

Who were these people and events and were they ordained by the Almighty God or the Fourth Beast? For example, God made male and female, which are husband and wife. There's a saying, and it's true, that God made Adam and Eve and not Adam and Steve. Some religions have adopted to marry two men and two women as husbands and wives. Who changed God's law of marriage? And who said that this country could have "freedom of religion," because God never told anyone that they had such options. You were to obey God, or you were dead, and those options still exist today.

DANIEL 7

In the first year of Belshazzar, king of Babylon Daniel had a dream and visions of his head upon his bed: then he wrote the dream and told the sum of the matters. Daniel spake and said, "I saw in my vision by night, and behold, the four winds of heaven strove upon the great sea. And four great beasts came up from the sea, diverse one from another. The first was like a lion and had eagle's wings: I beheld till the wings thereof were plucked, and it was lifted up from the earth, and made stand upon the feet as a man, and a man's heart was given to it.

And behold another beast, a second, like to a bear, and it raised up itself on one side, and it had three ribs in the mouth of it between the teeth of it: and they said thus unto it, Arise, devour much flesh.

After this I beheld, and lo another, like a leopard, which had upon the back of it four wings of a fowl; the beast had also four heads; and dominion was given to it.

After this I saw in the night visions, and behold a fourth beast, dreadful and terrible, and strong exceedingly; and it had great iron teeth: it devoured and brake in pieces, and stamped the residue with the feet of it: and it was diverse from all the beasts that were before it; and it had ten horns.

I considered the horns, and behold, there came up among them another little horn, before whom there were three of the first horns plucked up by the roots: and, behold, in this horn were eyes like the eyes of man, and a mouth speaking great things. [Horns represent authority and power like kings and rulers of countries. The number of horns indicates the number of countries you ruled over.]

I beheld till the thrones were cast down, and the Ancient of days did sit, whose garment was white as snow, and the hair of his head like the pure wool: his throne was like the fiery flame, and his wheels as burning fire. A fiery stream issued and came forth from before him: thousand ministered unto him, and ten thousand times ten thousand stood before him: the judgment was set, and the books were opened.

I beheld then because of the voice of the great words which the horn spake: I beheld even till the beast was slain, and his body destroyed, and given to the burning flame. As concerning the rest of the beasts, they had their dominion taken away: yet their lives were prolonged for a season and time.

I saw in the night visions, and behold, one like the Son of Man came with the clouds of heaven, and came to the Ancient of days, and they brought him near before him. And there was given him dominion, and glory, and a kingdom, that all people, nations, and languages, should serve him: his dominion is an everlasting dominion, which shall not pass away, and his kingdom that which shall not be destroyed. [Do you serve the Fourth Beast or Jesus Christ?]

I Daniel was grieved in my spirit in the midst of my body, and the visions of my head troubled me. I came near unto one of them that stood by, and asked him the truth of all this.

So, he told me, and made me know the interpretation of the things. These great beasts, which are four, are four kings, which shall arise out of the earth. But the saints of the most High shall take the kingdom, and possess the kingdom forever, even for ever and ever.

Then I would know the truth of the fourth beast, which was diverse from all the others, exceeding dreadful, whose teeth were of iron, and his nails of brass; which devoured, brake in pieces, and stamped the residue with his feet; and of the ten horns that were in his head, and of the other which came up, and before whom three fell; even of that horn that had eyes, and a mouth that spake very great things, whose look was more stout than his fellows. I beheld, and the same horn made war with the saints, and prevailed against them; until the Ancient of days came, and judgment was given to the saints of the most High; and the time came that the saints possessed the kingdom.

Thus, he said, "the fourth beast shall be the fourth kingdom upon earth, which shall be diverse from all kingdoms, and shall devour the whole earth, and shall tread it down, and break it in pieces. And the ten horns out of this kingdom are ten kings that shall arise: and another shall rise after them; and he shall be diverse from the first, and he shall subdue three kings. And he shall speak great words against the most High, and shall wear out the saints of the most High, and think to change times and laws: and they shall be given into his hand until a time and times and the dividing of time."

But the judgment shall sit, and they shall take away his dominion, to consume and to destroy it unto the end. And the kingdom and dominion, and the greatness of the kingdom under the whole heaven, shall be given to the people of the saints of the most High, whose kingdom is an everlasting kingdom, and all dominions shall serve and obey him.

Hitherto is the end of the matter. As for me Daniel, my cogitations much troubled me, and my countenance changed in me: but I kept the matter in my heart. (Daniel 7:1–28)

This should trouble the whole wide world in this dream because it troubled Daniel, a prophet of God, but—and I mean but—the world is not privy to this dream, only Daniel at this time. As I write, it is now 2021, and no one is *watching still.*

Also, Daniel always knew that the Jews had God in their life until this dream and that they could always call on God to help and to protect and to deliver them from captivity as he was on the day of the dream, but this would be no more due to the fourth Beast's power over the world until Jesus comes back. So, the whole world will be going in the direction of the Fourth Beast until Jesus comes back.

It's like coming out of the womb and the feet hit the ground, running right into the hands of the Beast, because it is his world now. It's like a trap that's been set, ready to snare, and you are *clueless* because the world seems okay: *I've got my job, my car, my family, my house, my education, vacations*—and you are in hell already and don't know it. Why? Because from coming out of the womb, you accept the world as it is and that it's okay. *The world isn't okay.*

The "righteousness of God" is unmatched by any spiritual or physical being that exists. in Genesis 1:3, God said "let there be light." Now unless God said it, you can't do it or change it. You know his word. You can't touch it, but you must obey it, "rightly dividing the word of truth." This is a way you can receive *the mark of the Beast or 666,* and the world is clueless because they aren't watching for the signs of the time like these people were watching.

Now when Jesus was born in Bethlehem of Judaea in the days of Herod the king, behold, there came wise men from the east to Jerusalem, saying, "Where is he that is born King of the Jews? For we have seen his star in the east, and are come to worship him." (Matthew 2:1–2)

"And this shall be a sign unto you; Ye shall find the baby wrapped in swaddling clothes, lying in a manger" (Luke 2:12). If the baby that the wise men sought had been born in a high-class hotel, then that wasn't Jesus, because that wasn't the sign. Jesus was to be born in a low-class hotel like a manger.

And behold, there was a man in Jerusalem, whose name was Simeon; and the same man was just and devout, waiting for the consolation of Israel: and the Holy Ghost was upon him. And it was revealed unto him by the Holy Ghost, that he should not see death, before he had seen the Lord's Christ. And he came by the Spirit into the temple: and when the parents brought in the child Jesus, to do for him after the custom of the law, then took he him up in his arms, and blessed God, and said,

"Lord, now lettest thou thy servant depart in peace, according to thy word: for mine eyes have seen thy salvation, which thou hast prepared before the face of all people; a light to lighten the Gentiles, and the glory of thy people Israel." (Luke 2:25–32)

BUT WHO IN THIS WORLD IS WATCHING FOR THE SIGNS Of TIME?

The Pharisees also with the Sadducees came, and tempting desired him that he would shew them a sign from heaven.

He answered and said unto them, "When it is evening, ye say, it will be fair weather: for the sky is red. And in the morning, it will be foul weather today: for the sky is red and lowering. O ye hypocrites, ye can discern the face of the sky; but can ye not discern the signs of the times?" (Matthew 16:1–3)

These are the signs of the time:

I will raise them up a Prophet from among the brethren, like unto thee, and will put my words in his mouth; and he shall speak unto them all that I shall command him, and it shall come to pass, that whosoever will not hearken unto my words which he shall speak in my name, I will require it of him. (Deuteronomy 18:18–19)

Rejoice greatly, O daughter of Zion; shout, O daughter of Jerusalem: behold, thy King cometh unto thee: he is just, and having salvation; lowly, and riding upon an ass colt the foal of an ass. (Zechariah 9:9)

Saying unto them, "Go into the village over against you, and straightway ye shall find an ass tied, and a colt with her: loose them and bring them unto me." (Matthew 21:2)

These people above that the Lord was talking to were living during the time of these prophecies, but they only had worldly knowledge, and they couldn't discern the times that they were standing in the presence of the Son of God just like the world today in 2021.

Do you see the signs of the time, readers?

Jesus is also in tune with His father in that He starts the day at "evening and then morning," never mentioning the term midnight to start a new day.

Jesus prophesied about a "religion" that was coming into great power and authority, the Fourth Beast. Tell me who he is talking about: "And call no man your father upon the earth: for one is your Father, which is in heaven" (Matthew 23:9). This is a "sign" from the Lord and cleverly imposed in the word so that only those who study and are *watching for the signs of time* can discern it. The Lord knows that there are earthly fathers, but there is only one heavenly and spiritual Father, which is the Almighty God and not a feeble-minded, carnal man who dies.

So, what religion calls their priests "father"? Then you will know who the Fourth Beast is.

AN EARTHLY IMITATION

" [He] opposeth and exalteth himself above all that is called God, or that is worshipped; so that he as God sitteth in the temple of God, shewing himself that he is God" (2 Thessalonians 2:4)

Who's watching? I will rant and rave over and over about this and many other scriptures through this book, so please be patient. I'm trying to put this all together for you that you may know where you are going.

Exodus 23:13 says, "And in all things that I have said unto you be circumspect: and make no mention of the name of other gods, neither let it be heard out of thy mouth." We say 'TGIF', but Friday is named after the so-called goddess Venus/Aphrodite/Freya. So, when you read the Book of Genesis, it has no idolatrous names because Genesis means "the beginning"; it's pure and righteous and holy, having no negative meaning, and God gave for dates all numbers from one to seven, and He rested.

In the process of time, He will give names of the months to his people Israel, but they will mean something spiritual and recall certain events that they need to remember like the Passover. *Please remember the Passover as you read this book.*

And the Lord spake unto Moses and Aaron in the land of Egypt saying, "This month shall be unto you the beginning of months: it shall be the first month of the year to you." (Exodus 12:1–2)

Deuteronomy 16:1 names this month Abib: "Observe the month of Abib, and keep the Passover unto the Lord thy God: for in the month of Abib the Lord thy God brought thee forth out of Egypt by night."

The months meant something *spiritual* and not *idolatrous* as the Fourth Beast's names for days and months would later mean. The instruction continues, now in Exodus 12:

Speak ye unto all the congregation of Israel, saying, "In the tenth day of this month they shall take to them every man a lamb, according to the house of their fathers, a lamb for an house: and if the household be too little for the lamb, let him and his neighbour next unto his house take it according to the number of the souls; every man according to his eating shall make your count for the lamb. Your lamb shall be without blemish, a male of the first year: ye shall take it out from the sheep, or from the goats: and ye shall keep it up until the fourteenth day of the same month: and the whole assembly of the congregation of Israel shall kill it in the evening. And they shall take of the blood, and strike it on the two side posts and on the upper door post of the houses, wherein they shall eat it. And they shall eat the flesh in that night, roast with fire, and unleavened bread; and with bitter herbs they shall eat it. Eat not of it raw, nor sodden at all with water, but roast with fire; his head with his legs, and with the purtenance thereof. And ye shall let nothing of it remain until the morning; and that which remaineth of it until the morning ye shall burn with fire. And thus, shall ye eat it; with your loins girded, your shoes on your feet, and your staff in your hand; and ye shall eat it in haste: it is the Lord's Passover."

For I will pass through the land of Egypt this night, and will smite all the firstborn in the land of Egypt, both man and beast; and against all the gods of Egypt I will execute judgment: I am the Lord. And the blood shall be to you for a token upon the houses where ye are: and when I see the blood, I will pass over you, and the plague shall not be upon you to destroy you, when I smite the land of Egypt.

And this day shall be unto you for a memorial; and ye shall keep it a feast to the Lord throughout your generations; ye shall keep it a feast by an ordinance forever. Seven days shall ye eat unleavened bread; even the first day ye shall put away leaven out of your houses: for whosoever eateth leavened bread from the first day until the seventh day, that soul shall be cut off from Israel. And in the first day there shall be a holy convocation, and in the seventh day there shall be an holy convocation to you; no manner of work shall be done in them, save that which every man must eat, that only may be done of you. (Exodus 12:3–16)

God is walking them through this as if they are two years old and to be truthful their minds are like those of two-year-old kids because this is the "caveman times of life."

Check this out how this is worded in Ezekiel 1:1–2: "Now it came to pass in the thirtieth year, in the fourth month, in the fifth day of the month, as I was among the captives by the river of Chebar, that the heavens were opened, and I saw visions of God. in the fifth day of the month, which was the fifth year of king Jehoiachin's captivity." There is no mention of idolatrous days or months, only references to the time when "The word of the LORD came expressly unto Ezekiel the priest" (vs. 3).

Ezekiel is written 1000 of years after the creation. In fact, there are no idolatrous names of days of the week or idolatrous names of the months in any of God's word. But who has changed God's days of the weeks and months of the year? The Fourth Beast.

If the Jews make a mistake, they paid with their lives. God didn't play with the Jews. "The letter killeth but the spirit keepth alive" (2 Corinthians 3:6). (Under the Old Testament there was little mercy, but under the New Testament there is mercy.)

Whatever name God attached to something or somebody, it always was positive and had a righteous meaning behind it. Some examples:

13

Neither shall thy name any more be called Abram, but thy name shall be Abraham; for a father of many nations have I made thee. (Genesis 17:5)

And he said, "thy name shall be called no more Jacob, but Israel: for as a prince hast thou power with God and with men, and hast prevailed." (Genesis 32:28)

And when they came to Marah, they could not drink of the waters of Marah, for they were bitter: therefore, the name of it was called Marah [meaning "bitter"]. (Exodus 15:23)

So, let's talk about time—or should I say, those names on the calendar. I was born in August, which is supposedly under the sign of Leo. Can you tell me where the day Sunday or the month August is found in the Bible? The times are there but not those familiar names; notice these scriptures once again:

And in all things that I have said unto you be circumspect: and make no mention of the name of other gods, neither let it be heard out of thy mouth. (Exodus 23:13)

"Don't even speak their names, period." Since three thousand years ago, God's language hasn't changed. Look at these New Testament passages, which don't mention the name Sunday. instead, they refer to the first day of the week, the day of the Lord's Supper, and the day of giving:

In the end of the Sabbath, as it began to dawn toward the first day of the week, came Mary Magdalene and the other Mary to see the sepulchre. (Matthew 28:1)

And upon the first day of the week, when the disciples came together to break bread, Paul preached unto them, ready to depart on the morrow; and continued his speech until midnight. (Acts 20:7)

Now concerning the collection for the saints, as I have given order to the churches of Galatia, even so do ye. Upon the first day of the week let every one of you lay by him in store, as God hath prospered him, that there be no gatherings when I come. (1 Corinthians 16:1–2)

The "first day of the week" is a day of worship, a "holy day." So why do we sin, calling it by an idolatrous name like "Sun Day"? This is how you get the "mark of the Beast," because *the Beast changed the times and laws of God.*

Why are these days on the Calendar? Because of the fourth Beast. Sun day because they worship the Sun god, Moon day (Monday) because they worship the Moon god and Tuesday (Mars/ Ares), Wednesday (Mercury/ Hermes), Thursday (Thor/ (Jupiter/ or (Zeus), Friday (Venus/ Aphrodite), and Saturday (Saturn/ Cronos) according to Wikipedia.

When thou art come into the land which the Lord thy God giveth thee, thou shalt not learn to do after the abominations of those nations. There shall not be found among you anyone that maketh his son or his daughter to pass through the fire, or that useth divination, or an observer of times, or an enchanter, or a witch. Or a charmer, or a consulter with familiar spirits, or a wizard, or a necromancer [palm readers and astrologers]. [Remember, I was born in August, and the "sign" is Leo, so where did the name *August* come from?] for all that do these things are an abomination unto the Lord: and because of these abominations the Lord thy God doth drive them out from before thee. (Deuteronomy 18:9–12)

God didn't want his people to be around such teachings, lest they be infected by their ideals. God is also "jealous" of other gods, as if they birth you instead of the invisible God.

Recall that early I said, *"Hell* can break loose"? Well, it has already:

Nay but, O man, who art thou that repliest against God? Shall the thing formed say to him that formed it, "Why hast thou made me thus?" (Romans 9:20)

I feel for God in this scripture. for example, imagine you are a parent whose kids will trust in their peers first or may call someone else their daddy. You know, I can relate to that. "I created you, but you're loving and obeying someone else." I had a neighbor who had a grandson that was living with my neighbor's mother and the grandson killed her for drugs. Can you feel it?

Honour thy father and thy mother: that thy days may be long upon the land which the Lord thy God giveth thee. (Exodus 20:12)

The Lord repeated this commandment from the Old Testament in the New Testament, in Colossians and Ephesians. The apostle Paul reiterated these scriptures some two thousand years ago. "Children, obey your parents in all things: for this is well pleasing unto the Lord" (Colossians 3:20). The Almighty God is saying to obey *Him* because *He* created you, not feeble, carnal-minded who sin and worship the fourth Beast.

Paul also repeats the command in Ephesians:

Children, obey your parents in the Lord: for this is right. Honour thy father and mother; (which is the first commandment with promise;) that it may be well with thee, and thou mayest live long on the earth. (Ephesians 6:1–3)

So, when the world disobeys its creator there are going to be some plagues, earthquakes, floods, famines, diseases, sickness, tsunamis, fires, tornadoes and the like. Why? Because God use the "elements" of the world to punish man—plagues, famine, hurricanes, fires, flooding, and the like.

At this also my heart trembleth, and is moved out of his place. Hear attentively the noise of his voice, and the sound that goeth out of his mouth. He directeth it under the whole heaven, and his lightning unto the ends of the earth. After it a voice roareth: he thundereth with the voice of his excellency; and he will not stay them when his voice is heard. God thundereth marvellously with his voice; great things doeth he, which we cannot comprehend. For he saith to the snow, Be thou on the earth; likewise to the small rain, and to the great rain of his strength. He sealeth up the hand of every man; that all men may know his work. Then the beasts go into dens, and remain in their places. Out of the south cometh the whirlwind: and cold out of the north. By the breath of God frost is given: and the breadth of the waters is straitened. Also, by watering he wearieth the thick cloud: he scattereth his bright cloud: And it is turned round about by his counsels: that they may do whatsoever he commandeth them upon the face of the world in the earth. He causeth it to come, whether for correction, or for his land, or for mercy. Hearken unto this, O Job: stand still, and consider the wondrous works of God. (Job 37:1–14)

Wow. God is especially jealous when you mention them every day of your life—Sunday, Monday, Tuesday, Wednesday, Thursday, Friday, and Saturday—and then the months: January, February, March, April, May, June, July, August, September, October, November, and December. (I try not to say these terms, *but you wouldn't know how to save your souls* if I didn't teach it.)

Why don't you try not saying them and see how it feels? But most important is that you are fighting the *Beast* to save your soul.

For example, your birthday is 7/22/1966. Now the days of the week are first day, second day, third day, the fourth day, fifth day, sixth day, and the seventh day and etc. You know, how does it feel to say, "*evening* and *morning*" and picture in your mind trying to understand truly when does the "*day* start and *end?*"

What about the months? How did the months of the year get their names? The months' names reflect a mix of gods and goddesses, rulers, and numbers. Discover how our calendar developed into what it is today.

CHAPTER SEVEN

HOW OUR CALENDAR CAME TO BE

The Ancient Roman Calendar

In the past, the world followed the Julian Calendar and today they follow the Gregorian Calendar, after Pope Gregory XIII in 1582, but it's these reforms were based on the ancient Roman calendar, believed to be invented by Romulus, who served as the first king of Rome around 753 BC. The Roman calendar, a complicated lunar calendar, had twelve months like our current calendar, but only ten of the months had formal names. Basically, winter was a "dead" period of time when the government and military wasn't active, so they only had names for the time period we think of as March through December.

March (Martius) was named for Mars, the god of war, because this was the month when active military campaigns resumed. May (Maius) and June (Junius) were also named for goddesses: Maia and Juno. April (Aprilis) is thought to stem from Latin aperio, meaning "to open"—a reference to the opening buds of springtime. The rest of the months were simply numbered; their original names in Latin meant the fifth (Quintilis), sixth (Sextilis), seventh (September), eighth (October), ninth (November), and tenth (December) month. Eventually, January (Januarius) and February (Februarius) were added to the end of the year, giving all twelve months proper names. January was named after Janus, the Roman god of beginnings and transitions, while February's name is believed to stem from Februa, an ancient festival dedicated to ritual springtime cleaning and washing.

Julian Calendar Updates

I believe these dates from the start of the Roman Calendar in the year 666.

When Julius Caesar became pontifex maximus, he reformed the Roman calendar so that the twelve months were based on Earth's revolutions around the Sun. It was a solar calendar, as we have today. January and February were moved to the front of the year, and leap years were introduced to keep the calendar year lined up with the solar year.

The winter months (January and February) remained a time of reflection, peace, new beginnings, and purification. After Caesar's death, the month Quintilis was renamed July in honor of Julius Caesar in 44 BC, and later, Sextilis was renamed August in honor of Roman emperor Augustus in 8 BC. Of course, all the renaming and reorganizing meant that some of the months' names no longer agreed with their position in the calendar (September to December, for example). Later emperors tried to name various months after themselves, but those changes did not outlive them.

Today's Gregorian Calendar

Quite a bit later, in 1582, Pope Gregory XIII introduced a number of reforms to the Julian calendar, as there were still some inaccuracies and adjustments to be made. Mainly, the Julian calendar had overestimated the amount of time it took the Earth to orbit the Sun, so the Gregorian calendar shortened the calendar year from 365.25 days to 365.2425 days. This meant that the calendar could be more easily corrected by leap years and that the dates of the equinoxes and solstices—and thus, the date of Easter— once again lined up with their observed dates.

If there be found among you, within any of thy gates which the Lord thy God giveth thee, man or woman, that hath wrought wickedness in the sight of the Lord thy God, in transgressing his covenant.

And hath gone and served other gods, and worshipped them, either the sun, or moon, or any of the host of heaven, which I have not commanded; And it be told thee, and thou hast heard of it, and enquired diligently, and, behold, it be true, and the thing certain, that such abomination is wrought in Israel: Then shalt thou bring fourth that man or that woman, which have committed that wicked thing, unto thy gates, even that man or that woman, and shalt stone them with stones, till they die. (Deuteronomy 17:2–5)

THE MARK OF THE BEAST: "666"

And he had power to give life unto the image of the beast, that the image of the beast should both speak, and cause that as many as would not worship the image of the beast should be killed. And he causeth all, both small and great, rich and poor, free and bond, to receive a mark in their right hand, or in their foreheads: and that no man might buy or sell, save he that had the mark, or the name of the beast, or the number of his name.

Here is wisdom. Let him that hath understanding count the number of the beast: for it is the number of a man; and his number is Six hundred threescore and six. (Revelation 13:15–18)

This is how you get the mark of the Beast (666) through "buying and selling": Easter, Christmas, Mother's Day and Father's Day, Ash Wednesday, the season of Lent, Saint Patrick's Day and Valentine's Day, Halloween and the like from the Julian calendar. Think "to change times and laws."

Once again, who are these people *on the calendar,* and who invented them? It was Rome, which is the Fourth Beast and who *crucified Jesus Christ.* The number "666" (from Wikipedia) means pre-Julian dates and laws because when Julius Caesar comes into power, he is going to adopt all of those idolatrous "Times and Laws" to his calendar, naming it the Julian Calendar and making sure that their number-one day is *Sun-day, the first day on the calendar,* and their number-one holiday is

Easter, which is celebrated every year on the first *Sun-day* following the first full moon after the spring equinox.

Revelation 13:18 says, "Here is wisdom. Let him that hath understanding count the number of the beast: for it is the number of a man; and his number is Six hundred threescore and six." *(Numbers are days,* and 666 are *days,* which equals times.) This is basically the start of the Roman calendar, which was implemented by *"the man,"* which is *Julius Caesar. Any Roman will have 666 because they implement the ideals of Rome.*

Different searches come up with different gods and goddesses, but it makes no difference *because* the Fourth Beast is *Rome,* if they liked your gods, they would worship them also. Rome had so many gods and goddesses that they became the *ultimate* Beast.

Now let's start with what's on the calendar like the days of the week.

1. Sunday, which is after the Romans' sun god, Apollo.

2. Monday or "Moonday" (Diana) which is after the Romans' moon god. Acts 19:27 says, "So that not only this our craft is in danger to be set at nought; but also, that the temple of the great goddess Diana should be despised, and her magnificence should be destroyed, whom all Asia and the world worshippeth."

3. Tuesday which is called Mars (Ares).

4. Wednesday is for the god Mercury.

5. Thursday is for Jupiter or Thor.

6. Friday is for Venus.

7. Saturday is for Saturn.

Now Let's Look at the Months

A Yahoo search defines the months.

The names of the months are all derived from three sources: Greek and Roman deities, Roman rulers, and numbers. Interestingly, though Julius Caesar made January the first month of the year with the implementation of the Julian Calendar in 709 BC, many places around the world continued to celebrate the New Year in March for centuries to come.

We see here a difference as to when the calendar was created, but God said that 666 was the number of a man, so let God be true and every man a liar. Something happened in the year 666, and it all points to Rome. But we are on the same page—just different years. "And it came to pass in those days, that there went out a decree from Caesar Augustus, that all the world should be taxed" (Luke 2:1).

(I was born in the month of August, and Leo is the "pagan" name and the astrological sign for that month.)

Easter represents *Rom's Main* Deity. The sole *etiology* of Rome's Julian calendar was to celebrate their goddess *Ester*, who was the goddess of fertility, and to make sure that that day would always fall on the third week in April by manipulation of the days on the calendar by watching the solar system.

Have you ever asked yourself, what do a rabbit and chicken eggs have to do with the death, burial, and resurrection of Jesus Christ? Rabbits and chicken eggs—do they even go together? A rabbit doesn't hatch eggs, but a chicken does—and the world is dumb. I mean, the world is simply clueless, really deceived. All of Rome's products of idols went to celebrate this idol called Easter, which is today a billion-dollar industry.

This is how you get the mark of the Beast—from "buying and selling" for the *Beast. Everything on the calendar is basically "buying and selling,"* dealing with *Rome's pagan holidays.* People are confused when they say "Easter" is in the Bible, but God put it there so that you may know who the Beast is, because the Jews were celebrating the Passover, but Rome was celebrating *"Easter."*

Once again in Exodus 12:21, we read about the Passover, "Then Moses called for all the elders of Israel, and said unto them, draw out and take you a lamb according to your families, and kill the Passover." The Passover was a Jewish feast celebrated by killing a "lamb or goat." The Passover was held in the first month, Abib. Now, with "Easter" you have a rabbit and chicken eggs.

Again we read in Leviticus 11:1–2, 6, "And the LORD spake unto Moses and to Aaron, saying unto them, Speak unto the children of Israel, saying, These are the beasts which ye shall eat among all the beasts that are on the earth … and the hare, because he cheweth the cud, but divideth not the hoof; he is unclean unto you." (A "hare" is a rabbit.)

Easter is in the fourth month, which is "April," and the Jews were celebrating the Passover, in which is in the first month, Abib. So, there is no way that the Jews ever celebrated the pagan holiday "Easter." The Jews hated Rome, and Rome hated the Jews.

THE "LAWS" OF ROME

Now about that time Herod the king stretched forth his hands to vex certain of the church. And he killed James the brother of John with the sword. And because he saw it pleased the Jews, he proceeded further to take Peter also. (Then were the days of unleavened bread.) (Acts 12:1–3)

Those days are connected with the Jewish Passover.

And he had power to give life unto the image of the beast, that the image of the beast should both speak, and cause that as many as would not worship the image of the beast should be killed. (Revelation 13:15)

Jesus, the apostles, and the disciples were all killed by Rome because they did not worship the Beast. Now what about you?

Acts 12:4 goes on from the previous passage to discuss Peter being put in prison: "And when he [Herod] had apprehended him [Peter], he put him in prison, and delivered him to four quaternions of soldiers to keep him; intending after Easter to bring him forth to the people." The Jewish Passover was in Abib, which is the first month of the year, and Rome's Easter obviously was in April which is the fourth month of the year. So, Peter was in prison for four months.

The Jews would not celebrate pagan holidays like Easter, and the Jews hated Rome. Easter was so holy in the mind of Herod that he wasn't going to kill the apostle Peter on that day. *Once again: Easter is*

Rome's pagan holiday and has nothing to do with the Jews. *The Lord's Supper* was instituted on the day of the *Passover*.

Now the first day of the feast of unleavened bread the disciples came to Jesus, saying unto him, "Where wilt thou that we prepare for thee to eat the Passover?" [No mention of the name Easter here. Why? Because Jesus and His disciples knew the scriptures about not mentioning the names of other gods.] And he said, "Go into the city to such a man, and say unto him, The Master saith, My time is at hand; I will keep the Passover at thy house with my disciples." And the disciples did as Jesus had appointed them; and they made ready the Passover. Now when the even [the time of sundown] was come, he sat down with the twelve. (Matthew 26:17–20)

Jesus never mentions the pagan name Easter during the Passover. Why? "And in all things that I have said unto you be circumspect: and make no mention of the name of other gods, neither let it be heard out of thy mouth" (Exodus 23:13). Jesus knew the Word of God, so He wasn't going to say or believe in this word *Easter*. Also remember that the Beast would kill anyone who didn't believe in his laws, so Jesus and the apostles were all killed by the Beast.

The whole world has their children involved in these pagan holidays like Halloween, which represents death. That's why you have witches, Frankenstein, ghosts, skulls, and black cats. Here's how God thinks about a witch: "Thou shalt not suffer a witch to live" (Exodus 22:18). *And why is the black cat a similitude of evil* (Rome)? Why does the term black seem to convey the sense of darkness and mystery, as in black plague, black cats, Black Sunday, Black Friday, and the like?

And God said, "Let the earth bring forth the living creature after his kind, cattle, and creeping thing, and beast of the earth after his kind": and it was so. And God made the beast of the earth after his kind, and cattle after their kind, and everything that creepeth upon the earth after his kind: and God saw that it was good. (Genesis 1:24–25)

"It was good." So, who said that the black cat was evil or mysterious when the almighty God said it was good? Rome believed that black was dark, evil, and mysterious. If you study that, Rome never went into the *deepest parts of Africa.* Rome conquered the top parts of Africa because maybe in their minds the Africans were—get this now—*uncivilized.* The word civilization was invented by, you guessed it, the Fourth Beast: Rome.

Remember now, Rome—*who crucified the Son of God,* killed the apostles, and would crucify at one time as many as six thousand men and called man all kinds of names like *nigger, spick, Jap, slant-eyed, savage, wetback,* and the like—could call somebody *uncivilized.*

I was watching a TV show and heard the phrase drawn and quartered and said, "What does that mean?" So, I looked it up and from my understanding that it was a form of punishment where the person was tied down on something like a wooden pallet and paraded around the city, then was hanged almost to death and taken down and cut up into "QUARTERS" and then those quarters would be hung around the city. And you call us *uncivilized?*

Rome invented the term civilization, so we live in today's society dominated by Rome's ideals. Get this now: the whites who hanged African slaves, took their lands, burned crosses in their yards, stole their inventions, and raped them, had the nerve to call the Indians savages. All this is the laws of Rome.

Contrast that with the laws of God.

Master, which is the great commandment in the law?

Jesus said unto him, "Thou shalt love the Lord thy God with all thy heart, and with all thy soul, and with all thy mind. This is the first and great commandment. And the second is like unto it, Thou shalt love thy neighbour as thyself." On these two commandments hang all the law and the prophets. (Matthew 22:36–40)

And in Matthew 7:12 Jesus said, "Therefore all things whatsoever ye would that men should do to you, do ye even so to them: for this is the law and the prophets."

CHRISTMAS OR CHRIST MASS

"My Lord, forgive me for using your holy name in this way."

Romulus killed his brother Remus to take over Rome, and civilization's murderous existence began with the two of them being suckled by a she-wolf. How can the world believe in such *paganism*, such **fables**, such *legends*, and such *mythology* and observe those things on the calendar?

I went to get my driver's license and was turned around and was told to go and get my birth certificate. Now, your birth certificate has your date of birth, place of birth, the time, male or female, your parents, and the doctor's or midwife's. We know that Jesus was born in Bethlehem in a manger, and that there were three wise men with gifts, and that someone would try to kill him at birth, and all of this was done by prophecy, but nowhere in the scriptures is the actual date of birth for Jesus Christ. "What day, month, and year was the time of the Savior's birth?"

Now think: don't you know that the Creator of all living things in heaven and on earth and who established time in the beginning—numbering the days and establishing the months—wouldn't you think that the almighty Jehovah (I'm not a Jehovah's witness) would know the day of birth for His only Son? How is this then? Revelation 12:9 tells us, "And the great dragon was cast out, that old serpent, called the Devil, and Satan, which deceiveth the whole world: he was cast out into the earth, and his angels were cast out with him."

HAVE YOU BEEN DECEIVED?

John 8:44

"Ye are of your father the devil, and the lusts of your father ye will do. He was a murderer from the beginning, and abode not in the truth, because there is no truth in him. When he speaketh a lie, he speaketh of his own: for he is a liar, and the father of it" (John 8:44).

You say it was December 25? Ah, in what year was the Savior born? first of all, *December is an idolatrous month,* and there is no month in the bible called December. Remember, God never used idolatrous names for months. So, all of that is a *white lie.* Remember, there's no such thing as a "black lie," only a white lie. This supposedly would take away the severity of telling a lie, which can take you to hell. There is a "White Christmas" but not a "Black Christmas." A white Santa Claus, not a black Santa Claus, will come down your chimney, even when you don't have one like me as a little boy. This Santa had a workshop full of elves, and he traveled by a sled that's led by a reindeer with a red, shiny nose. On this day he will deliver gifts to the whole wide world, from the North Pole to the South Pole in one night on a reindeer-driven sled.

ROME was full of such *fables* and *mythological* gods and goddesses. "But refuse profane and old wives' fables and exercise thyself rather unto godliness" (1 Timothy 4:7). You must understand that some of the Bible was written at a time of some of the world's greatest philosophers like: Plato, Socrates, and Aristotle. You also had the Stoics and the Epicureans. These groups of people for the most part was trying to figure out how the world began, because God gave them no wisdom. So, their philosophy was to "eat, drink, and be merry, for tomorrow we die."

Here's what God said, through Paul, in answer to the philosophers: "Then certain philosophers of the Epicureans, and of the Stoicks, encountered him. And some said, what will this babbler say? Other some, He seemeth to be a setter forth of strange gods: because he preached unto them Jesus, and the resurrection" (Acts 17:18). This was the world's "wisdom" at that time. "Beware lest any man spoil you through philosophy and vain deceit, after the tradition of men, after the rudiments of the world, and not after Christ" (Colossians 2:8).

CHRISTMAS TREE

I dolatry was so bad in that world some three thousand years ago and is even now in 2021. Have you ever sung the song "Oh Christmas Tree, oh Christmas Tree"? You do know that you're singing to a tree that someone cut down or manufactured, right? Then you deck it with gold and silver ornamentations. Check this out:

Hear ye the word which the LORD speaketh unto you, O house of Israel: Thus, saith the LORD, learn not the way of the heathen, and be not dismayed at the signs of heaven; for the heathen are dismayed at them. For the customs of the people are vain: for one cutteth a tree out of the forest, the work of the hands of the workman, with the axe. They deck it with silver and with gold; they fasten it with nails and with hammers, that it move not. They are upright as the palm tree, but speak not: they must need be borne, because they cannot go. Be not afraid of them; for they cannot do evil, neither also is it in them to do good. Forasmuch as there is none like unto thee, O LORD; thou art great, and thy name is great in might. (Jeremiah 10:1–6)

Heathen refers to anyone who is not a Jew, and the command not to be "dismayed at the signs of heaven" is a reference to astrology or stargazers. in other words, don't do as the world does. The Jews had a caveman- like mind, and God was trying his best to keep the Jews from following the countries around them. The heathen or Gentiles or the world (they are all the same people) would go into the forest and cut down a tree. Then they would fashion it however they wanted, to look like a man, woman, or animal, and then deck it down with real silver and gold. Guess what? The "idol" couldn't even move, talk, walk, hear, or speak, but they believed in it and worshipped it and even would sell it. God warned his people not to be afraid of this, because this is how cave-minded the Jews were as well as the idolaters themselves. Now go cut down a "Christmas tree."

CHRISTMAS

You have no clue how much I hate to say this word because it is *blasphemous* and *sacrilegious* to use the holy name of Jesus with this suffix: -*mas.*

And he opened his mouth in blasphemy against God, to blaspheme his name, and his tabernacle, and them that dwell in heaven. And it was given unto him to make war with the saints, and to overcome them: and power was given him over all kindreds, and tongues, and nations. And all that dwell upon the earth shall worship him, whose names are not written in the book of life of the Lamb slain from the foundation of the world.

If any man have an ear, let him hear.

He that leadeth into captivity shall go into captivity: he that killeth with the sword must be killed with the sword. Here is the patience and the faith of the saints.

And I beheld another beast coming up out of the earth; and he had two horns like a lamb, and he spake as a dragon. [(This imposter is acting like Jesus, the Lamb of God, but he is the devil, that old dragon, that deceiveth the world in the form of a man.).

How can a lamb speak like a dragon? Remember that Jesus said they come in sheep's clothing, but inwardly they are wolves, which are false teachers.] And he exerciseth all the power of the first beast before him, and causeth the earth and them which dwell therein to worship the first beast, whose deadly wound was healed. And he doeth great wonders, so that he maketh fire come down from heaven on the earth in the sight of men, (Revelation 13:6–13)

The Roman Catholic Church has *mass,* and they are the ones who invented this idea called Christ-Mas or Xmas and this fabulistic character named Santa Claus, dressed in a red and white suit. This is a billion- dollar business, you know, buying and selling and receiving the *mark of the Beast.* They also *crucified* my Savior Jesus Christ. You've *added* a name -*mas* that is so satanic and devilish from Rome to the holy and righteous name of Jesus Christ.

ADDING TO THE WORD OF GOD

D euteronomy 4:2 says, "Ye shall not add unto the word which I command you, neither shall ye diminish ought from it, that ye may keep the commandments of the LORD your God which I command you."

Proverbs 30:5 says, "Every word of God is pure: he is a shield unto them that put their trust in him"—in His words and not feeble-minded, carnal man's words or ideals.

Revelation 22:18–19 says, "For I testify unto every man that heareth the words of the prophecy of this book, if any man shall add unto these things, God shall add unto him the plagues that are written in this book: and if any man shall take away from the words of the book of this prophecy, God shall take away his part out of the book of life, and out of the holy city, and from the things which are written in this book." Rome is under a curse, along with the rest of the world. *Remember what happened to Pompeii!*

The world is going to be about everyone's everyday lives, buying and selling, when the Lord comes back and catches the world off guard and unprepared, and all hell is going to break loose: "But the day of the Lord will come as a thief in the night; in the which the heavens shall pass away with a great noise, and the elements shall melt with fervent heat, the earth also and the works that are therein shall be burned up" (2 Peter 3:10).

But of the times and the seasons, brethren, ye have no need that I write unto you. For yourselves know perfectly that the day of the Lord so cometh as a thief in the night. For when they shall say, Peace and safety; then sudden destruction cometh upon them, as travail upon a woman with child; and they shall not escape. But ye, brethren, are not in darkness, that that day should overtake you as a thief. (1 Thessalonians 5:1–4)

But today, in 2021, the world is in the *darkness of hell* and is *clueless*.

And to you who are troubled [God will give] rest with us, when the Lord Jesus shall be revealed from heaven with his mighty angels, in flaming fire taking vengeance on them that know not God, and that obey not the gospel of our Lord Jesus Christ: who shall be punished with everlasting destruction from the presence of the Lord, and from the glory of his power. (2 Thessalonians 1:7–9)

So, when you say the ROMAN CATHOLIC CHURCH, BAPTIST CHURCH, JEHOVAH WITNESS, SEVENTH DAY ATVINTIST CHURCH, METHODIST CHURCH, AME Zion Methodist, Christian Scientist, illuminati, Scientology, Episcopal, Presbyterian, Muslim, Jewish, Mormons, The Holiness Congregations, and the like—you have added to the name of Jesus Christ's wife's name, which is the *Church*. None of these names for churches are in the Bible to belong to.

When I used to talk to people about the Lord, I would ask, "What faith or belief or congregation do you belong to?" and they would say one of these names above. Romans 10:17 says, "Faith cometh by hearing, and hearing by the word of God." So where in the word of God do you hear these names to believe in or to be a part of worshipping the almighty God? Names such as the Roman Catholic Church, Lutherans, the Baptist Church, Jehovah's Witnesses, Seventh-Day Adventist Church, Methodist Church, AME Zion Methodist, Christian Scientist, illuminati, Scientology, Episcopal, Presbyterian, Muslim, Jewish, Mormons, the Holiness religions, and the like. Take out your Bible and find the names as written, and you will see that they aren't there because they fall under the category of *false teachers*.

THE TELEVANGELISTS

Jesus said, "For many shall come in my name, saying, I am Christ; and shall deceive many" (Matthew 24:5). God tricked the whole wide world by deceiving them Himself because of unbelief.

Consider 2 Thessalonians 2:1–12:

Now we beseech you, brethren, by the coming of our Lord Jesus Christ, and by our gathering together unto him, that ye be not soon shaken in mind, or be troubled, neither by spirit, nor by word, nor by letter as from us, as that the day of Christ is at hand. Let no man deceive you by any means: for that day shall not come, except there come a falling away first, and that man of sin be revealed, the son of perdition [the Antichrist]; who opposeth and exalteth himself above all that is called God, or that is worshipped; so that he as God sitteth in the temple of God, shewing himself that he is God.

Remember ye not, that, when I was yet with you, I told you these things? And now ye know what withholdeth that he might be revealed in his time. For the mystery of iniquity doth already work: only he who now letteth will let, until he be taken out of the way. And then shall that Wicked be revealed, whom the Lord shall consume with the spirit of his mouth, and shall destroy with the brightness of his coming: even him, whose coming is after the working of Satan with all power and signs and lying wonders, and with all deceivableness of unrighteousness in them that perish; because they received not the love of the truth, that they might be saved. And for this cause God shall send them strong delusion, that they should believe a lie: that they all might be damned who believed not the truth, but had pleasure in unrighteousness.

The Roman Catholics believe in "praying to Mary" who was the mother of Jesus. Mary is holy, but the Catholics give her a bad name. Mary is holy in her own right because the Almighty God chose her to be the mother of Jesus, and that's where it ends. Jesus, not Mary, is the intercessor between God and man.

This is called "the spirit of antichrist" when you put Mary before Jesus when praying. "And whatsoever ye shall ask in my name, that will I do, that the father may be glorified in the Son" (John 14:13)—not in Mary's name. "Wherefore he is able also to save them to the uttermost that come unto God by him, seeing he ever liveth to make intercession for them" (Hebrews 7:25); Mary isn't a "he".

Jesus died on the cross, not Mary. "But he was wounded for our transgressions, he was bruised for our iniquities: the chastisement of our peace was upon him; and with his stripes we are healed" (Isaiah 53:5).

Now there stood by the cross of Jesus his mother, and his mother's sister, Mary the wife of Cleophas, and Mary Magdalene. When Jesus therefore saw his mother, and the disciple standing by, whom he loved, he saith unto his mother, Woman, behold thy son! Then saith he to the disciple, Behold thy mother! And from that hour that disciple took her unto his own home. (John 19:25–27)

Jesus, not Mary, was prophesied to save the world. "For God so loved the world, that he gave his only begotten Son, that whosoever believeth in him should not perish, but have everlasting life" (John 19:25-27).

Praying on Rosary beads is a form of *idolatry*. What about the "hail Mary pass" in football? Just like "Hail Caesar" and "Heil Hitler"—

sound familiar? So, to put the Roman Catholics' *unholy name -mas or mass* to the holy name of Jesus Christ is an *abomination* to God.

Doing this causes the Roman Catholics to be the Antichrist, which makes the "pope" the Son of Perdition. So, to add to the name of *the holy Son of God, which is "Jesus Christ," is a great sin.*

When I was stationed at the American Embassy in Bonn, Germany, as a Marine Security Guard, I had to take a hundred hours of instruction in the German Language. My teacher was an elderly beautiful person, and I asked her how she felt about Hitler, and she said they hated him. This brings me to my next point about a man named Erich Priebke.

I saw on YouTube that Erich Priebke was a Nazi officer during the Hitler regime who had a part in killing millions of Jews. After the Allies took over, he and others like him escaped to I believe Argentina and there obtained new identities. At this time there are Jews who seek out these types of people and they found him, but they needed help from a US Anchorman to seal his fate. Priebke was being hidden by the Roman Catholics. This shows the difference between Rome's laws and the almighty God's laws, switching to "hating thy neighbor" from "loving thy neighbor."

I also remember when in Bonn seeing some cathedrals and castles. I had a chance to go to a ceremony at a Catholic organization and when entering felt "eerie" at hearing the organs and the operatic singing. I didn't understand any of the ceremony because sometimes the priest would speak in Latin, and they had these praying benches, and every minute you would be kneeling to pray. By the time you got up from kneeling, it was time to get back down, and this wore me out at nineteen years of age. Now, I had a bad back and I wasn't going to get bad knees, so I never went back. Thank God. Jesus said, "But when ye pray, use not vain repetitions, as the heathen do: for they think that they shall be heard for their much speaking" (Matthew 6:7). Up and down, up and down …

And God spake all these words, saying,

"I am the Lord thy God, which have brought thee out of the land of Egypt, out of the house of bondage."

Thou shalt have no other gods before me.

Thou shalt not make unto thee any graven image, or any likeness of anything that is in heaven above, or that is in the earth beneath, or that is in the water under the earth. Thou shalt not bow down thyself to them, nor serve them: for I the Lord thy God am a jealous God, visiting the iniquity of the fathers upon the children unto the third and fourth generation of them that hate me; [When you believe in these idols you hate God.] and shewing mercy unto thousands of them that love me, and keep my commandments. (Exodus 20:1–6)

The world would ask, "Who's your idol?" I was a collector of vintage items, and I got caught up in "I found something great, and I'm going to make a lot of money," which was a devilish mindset, and I had to get rid of them. I don't want the mark of the Beast. Covetousness, which is greed, is also idolatry. Romans 7:7 teaches, "What shall we say then? Is the law a sin? God forbid. Nay, I had not known sin, but by the law: for I had not known lust, except the law had said, thou shalt not covet."

Jesus said unto him, "It is written again, thou shalt not tempt the Lord thy God."

Again, the devil taketh him up into an exceeding high mountain, and sheweth him all the kingdoms of the world, and the glory of them; and saith unto him, all these things will I give thee, if thou wilt fall down and worship me [fame and glory].

Then saith Jesus unto him, get thee hence, Satan: for it is written, Thou shalt worship the Lord thy God, and him only shalt thou serve. (Matthew 4:7–10)

In today's society man is selling his soul to the devil for gain.

This scripture comes to mind.

And when he had called the people unto him with his disciples also, he said unto them, "Whosoever will come after me, let him deny himself, and take up his cross, and follow me. For whosoever will save his life shall lose it; but whosoever shall lose his life for my sake and the gospel's, the same shall save it. For what shall it profit a man, if he shall gain the whole world, and lose his own soul? Or what shall a man give in exchange for his soul? Whosoever therefore shall be ashamed of me and of my words in this adulterous and sinful generation; of him also shall the Son of man be ashamed, when he cometh in the glory of his father with the holy angels." (Mark 8:34–38)

The "mark of the Beast" is a spiritual mark on your soul; only God knows that you have it, and only God can remove it. Satan wants everyone to go to hell, so he's happy that you have the mark. The mark is not 666 on your forehead of course God wants you to think to get to heaven because it's symbolism and I believe it's God's way of weaning out those that don't want to fight to figure it out by studying the Bible to get to heaven.

Remember, Paul told Timothy to "study to shew thyself approve unto God, a workman that needeth not to be ashamed, rightly dividing the word of truth". (2 Timothy 2:15).

People study to be doctors, lawyers, engineers, and politicians for many years.

You ever go into a doctor's office and see all of their degrees hanging on the walls? And what about attorneys and TV commercials, trying to get your business, with all of those legal books behind them?

Remember, I said to *think* because it's how you believe in this life; you know where your brain is and your hands carry out the crime of your belief. This whole world is greedy with "buying and selling" to support the Beast's *agenda*.

DID YOU KNOW?

Did you know that the stock market was originally started by the Dutch, according to Wikipedia, and that the Dutch sold slaves at the beginning? You know— *"buying and selling"* man for unjust gain.

To believe in the Beast's ideals, which are against God, is how you get the mark. God put a mark on Cain for killing his brother, Abel, so that whoever saw him knew that there was something wrong with this man and they wouldn't kill him. Now that may have been a physical mark of some sort, but who really knows? People are walking around today not knowing that they have the mark of the Beast. "And the LORD said unto him, therefore whosoever slayeth Cain, vengeance shall be taken on him sevenfold. And the LORD set a mark upon Cain, lest any finding him should kill him" (Genesis 4:15). Some people are born with birthmarks, or was it some form of a creed put upon Cain? Who really knows but God, the devil, and Cain?

Everything I write is up for debate, but only truth shall prevail. When you put it all together, only those that are destined will know that this is the truth, but those who are entrenched in the Beast will fight truth. "Sanctify them through thy truth: thy word is truth" (John 17:17). There is no lie in truth. Jesus was asking His father to separate the apostles from the world because they were holy men of God.

"Faith cometh by hearing, and hearing by the word of God" (Romans 10:17). (We obtain our faith by believing in the word of God and not man, the Beast.)

"God forbid": yea, let God be true, but every man a liar; that thou mightest be justified in thy sayings, and mightiest overcome when thou art judged," (Romans 3:4). "Study to shew thyself approved unto God, a workman that needeth not to be ashamed, rightly dividing the word of truth" (2 Timothy 2:15). There is an Old Truth (the Old Testament, written only for the Jewish nation) and a New Truth (the New Testament, written for the whole world). The first pertained to the Jews in their time (BCE), and the other pertains to the world after the cross (AD). *Study so you don't* receive the mark. This world studies to be doctors, lawyers, engineers, politicians, and the like, only to miss out on heaven because they studied the wrong books for all of those years.

STUDY THE OLD TESTAMENT FOR EXAMPLES

The reasons we still study the Old Testament are cited in 1 Corinthians 10.

Moreover, brethren, I would not that ye should be ignorant, how that all our fathers were under the cloud, and all passed through the sea; and were all baptized unto Moses in the cloud and in the sea; and did all eat the same spiritual meat; and did all drink the same spiritual drink: for they drank of that spiritual Rock that followed them: and that Rock was Christ. But with many of them God was not well pleased: for they were overthrown in the wilderness.

Now these things were our examples, to the intent we should not lust after evil things, as they also lusted [rightly dividing the *word of truth*]. Neither be ye idolaters, as were some of them; as it is written, the people sat down to eat and drink, and rose up to play. Neither let us commit fornication [having sex without being married], as some of them committed, and fell in one day three and twenty thousand. Neither let us tempt Christ, as some of them also tempted, and were destroyed of serpents. Neither murmur ye, as some of them also murmured, and were destroyed of the destroyer [to speak against God and His *Word*].

Now all these things happened unto them for ensamples: and they are written for our admonition, upon whom the ends of the world are come. (1 Corinthians 10:1–11)

The Transfiguration

And there appeared unto them Elias with Moses: and they were talking with Jesus. …

And there was a cloud that overshadowed them: and a voice came out of the cloud, saying, "This is my beloved Son: hear him." (Mark 9:4, 7)

You have Elias, the great prophet, and Moses, the great Lawgiver, they both spoke of the coming of Jesus Christ and His great authority and power and God the father giving them witness to that.

And Jesus came and spake unto them, saying, "All power is given unto me in heaven and in earth. Go ye therefore, and teach all nations, baptizing them in the name of the father, and of the Son, and of the Holy Ghost: teaching them to observe all things whatsoever I have commanded you: and, lo, I am with you always, even unto the end of the world. Amen." (Matthew 28:18–20)

"Teaching them to observe all things whatsoever I have commanded you." The apostles never taught the days and months or the holidays on the calendar. Have you checked your "horoscope" this morning to start your day off right to *hell*?

"And in all things that I have said unto you be circumspect [check out your whole life prudently according to my words]: and make no mention of the name of other gods, neither let it be heard out of thy mouth" (Exodus 23:13). Not even something so seemingly innocent as "TGIF." When I was a Marine Security Guard for the American embassies, we had this day called TGIF. On this pagan day called "Friday," embassy personnel from the American, German, British, Canadian, and visitors would come to the "Marine House" and party like at a local club. The proceeds would go towards our Marine Corps ball, and sometimes the ambassador would show up. "In God we trust, all others pay." When it comes to money in America, someone will pay but with their souls. Who told America to put God's name on carnal paper money? America enslaved a culture, the Africans, and lynched them, sometimes five or ten at a time at barbecues, while the little white kids looked up at them being hanged. Rome was known at times to crucify up to six thousand people at once.

Remember now, every day of your life when you say the days of the week and months of the year and celebrate the holidays on the calendar, this is idolatry. God said don't even mention it out of your mouth. All of the holidays are for idolatrous gains of "buying and selling." There are Easter eggs and chocolates and Easter outfits and baskets. There's Saint Valentine's Day; who was he because God never mentions him in the Bible? And Saint Patricks' Day—you know, "Don't forget to wear green," or you will get pinched." What does green have to do with worshipping God? Not to mention Santa Claus. These are billion-dollar industries from "buying and selling."

And he doeth great wonders, so that he maketh fire come down from heaven on the earth in the sight of men, and deceiveth them that dwell on the earth by the means of those miracles which he had power to do in the sight of the beast; saying to them that dwell on the earth, that they should make an image to the beast, which had the wound by a sword, and did live. And he had power to give life unto the image of the beast, that the image of the beast should both speak, and cause that as many as would not worship the image of the beast should be killed. And he causeth all, both small and great, rich and poor, free and bond, to receive a mark in their right hand, or in their foreheads: and that no man might buy or sell, save he that had the mark, or the name of the beast, or the number of his name.

Here is wisdom. Let Him that hath understanding count the number of the beast: for it is the number of a man; and his number is Six hundred threescore and six. (Revelation 13:13–18)

Do you have the mark?

For a certain man named Demetrius, a silversmith, which made silver shrines for Diana, brought no small gain unto the craftsmen; whom he called together with the workmen of like occupation, and said, "Sirs, ye know that by this craft we have our wealth. Moreover ye see and hear, that not alone at Ephesus, but almost throughout all Asia, this Paul hath persuaded and turned away much people, saying that they be no gods, which are made with hands: so that not only this our craft is in danger to be set at nought; but also that the temple of the great goddess Diana should be despised, and her magnificence should be destroyed, whom all Asia and the world worshippeth."

And when they heard these sayings, they were full of wrath, and cried out, saying, "Great is Diana of the Ephesians." And the whole city was filled with confusion: and having caught Gaius and Aristarchus, men of Macedonia, Paul's companions in travel, they rushed with one accord into the theatre. And when Paul would have entered in unto the people, the disciples suffered him not. (Acts 19:24–30)

This is how you get the mark of the Beast (666) through "buying and selling": Easter, Christmas, Mother's Day and Father's Day, Ash Wednesday, the yearly Lent, Saint Patrick's and Valentine's Day, Halloween, and the like.

Once again who are these people on the calendar, and who invented them? Rome, which is the fourth Beast and crucified Jesus Christ. The number 666 means pre-Julian dates and laws, because when Julius Caesar came into power, he was going to adopt all of those idolatrous times and laws to his calendar, naming it the Julian calendar and making sure that the number-one holiday is Easter, celebrated every year in springtime.

"AS AN AFRICAN"

A s Africans, we took on our masters' names. My daddy was named "Julius." We also took on their religions: Catholic, Baptist, Methodist (AME Zion), Jehovah's Witnesses, Mormons, Episcopal, Presbyterian, Jewish, Muslims, illuminati, Christian Scientist, Scientology, Buddha, Seventh-Day Adventist, Holiness religions, and the like. Most of these religions did not want a black in them, so the Africans they copied the white religions by not having a religion of their own.

My question to the African community is, what made you think once again that the whites had the answers for your salvation? In other words, what made you as a person think that they were the only people who knew how to be saved? You are copying the Beast ignorantly and will receive the mark of the Beast—666. You know, they lied to you, they made you slaves, raised taxes on you, lynched you, stole your property, didn't give you bank loans, burned crosses in your yards, repossessed your properties, raped you, stole your patents, didn't give you fair wages, called you Nigger, and took away your ancestry—and you want to copy them?

I say again, "What made you think that they knew how to get to heaven when that same Bible they toted said, "Love thy neighbor as thy self? Were we not neighbors? But the stranger that dwelleth with you shall be unto you as one born among you, and thou shalt love him as thyself; for ye were strangers in the land of Egypt: I am the Lord your God" (Leviticus 19:34—almost four thousand years ago).

Jesus said, "For many shall come in my name, saying, I am Christ; and shall deceive many" (Matthew 24:5). My question to you is, "Where are they? If you were the original Creator of time, why would your months and dates change?

DESTINY

Your destiny is because you don't study the Word of God but study the word of man. Hosea 4:6 says, "My people are destroyed for lack of knowledge: because thou hast rejected knowledge, I will also reject thee, that thou shalt be no priest to me: seeing thou hast forgotten the law of thy God, I will also forget thy children."

The world knows what it takes to be a president, a doctor, a lawyer, an engineer, a teacher. Some of these jobs take a lifetime to fulfill. Then where is the "time" for the Lord, who can put your soul away forever?

The average life of man is threescore and ten, which is seventy years because a score is twenty years, so God is giving man seventy years to figure this out, give or take some years. (Psalms 90:10).

So why you are studying for the world, only to live to be seventy? I would be studying to live forever with God if I were you. People must work, but please prioritize your life, and put the Lord first. Daniel 7:17 explains Daniel's vision in part by saying, "These great beasts, which are four, are four kings, which shall arise out of the earth." Let's look again at the vision itself.

Daniel spake and said, "I saw in my vision by night, and behold, the four winds of the heaven strove upon the great sea. And four great beasts came up from the sea, diverse one from another. The first was like a lion, and had eagle's wings: I beheld till the wings thereof were plucked, and it was lifted up from the earth, and made stand upon the feet as a man, and a man's heart was given to it." (Daniel 7:2–4)

The lion: According to Wikipedia, that was the "Median" kingdom or the Medes, who took over the earth. Their empire was established in 679–549 BC. Today they are Iran.

And behold another beast, a second, like to a bear, and it raised up itself on one side, and it had three ribs in the mouth of it between the teeth of it: and they said, "thus unto it, Arise, devour much flesh." (Daniel 7:5)

The bear: Persia, which is akin to Media, took over the world from 559 to 331 BCE, according to National Geographic.

After this I beheld, and lo another, like a leopard, which had upon the back of it four wings of a fowl; the beast had also four heads; and dominion was given to it. (Daniel 7:6)

The leopard: This is when Alexander the Great of Greece took over the world from Persia in the period 336–323 BCE, according to Wikipedia.

After this I saw in the night visions, and behold a fourth beast, dreadful and terrible, and strong exceedingly; and it had great iron teeth: it devoured and brake in pieces and stamped the residue with the feet of it: and it was diverse from all the beasts that were before it; and it had ten horns. (Daniel 7:7)

By now, if you took any history classes in school and you paid attention, you know that the fourth beast is the Roman Empire, but you don't know that the fourth beast is Rome because the history books stay away from God, not knowing the Word of God, and they can't tie these things together. As a result, you are to know more of the "world" than you know of God. Why? Because church and state laws and many different religions (false teachers) have kept us from truth. This is by design of Satan and the fourth beast. Yes, they work hand in hand. "Let them alone: they be blind leaders of the blind. And if the blind lead the blind, both shall fall into the ditch," Jesus said in Matthew 15:14.

THE POPE

D id you know the name Pope means father? This is the name given to every top spiritual leader over the life of the Catholic Organization which is the fourth beast according to Daniel. Even in movies the basic priest of the Catholic Organization is called father. Jesus Christ as he walks and talks to his disciples one day prophesied warning about this term father and he said, "Call no man father upon the earth for one is your father which is in heaven."

So, the Lord said not to call any man Father in a spiritual setting or confessions, but you have about 1.4 billion Catholics that disobey the Lord who's going to judge them for this.

Matthew 23:7-12

7　　And greetings in the markets, and to be called of men, Rabbi, Rabbi.

8　　But be not ye called Rabbi: for one is your Master, even Christ; and all ye are brethren.

9　　And call no man your father upon the earth: for one is your Father, which is in heaven.

10　　Neither be ye called masters: for one is your Master, even Christ.

11　　But he that is greatest among you shall be your servant.

12　　And whosoever shall exalt himself shall be abased; and he that shall humble himself shall be exalted. The exaltation of man on the earth to liken himself to the Almighty God is blasphemous.

In Mark 2:1-12

1. And again, he entered into Capernaum after some days; and it was noised that he was in the house.

2. And straightway many were gathered together, insomuch that there was no room to receive them, no, not so much as about the door: and he preached the word unto them.

3. And they come unto him, bringing one sick of the palsy, which was borne of four.

4. And when they could not come nigh unto him for the press, they uncovered the roof where he was: and when they had broken it up, they let down the bed wherein the sick of the palsy lay.

5. When Jesus saw their faith, he said unto the sick of the palsy, Son, thy sins be forgiven thee.

6. But there was certain of the scribes sitting there, and reasoning in their hearts,

7. Why doth this man thus speak blasphemies? who can forgive sins but God only?

8. And immediately when Jesus perceived in his spirit that they so reasoned within themselves, he said unto them, "Why reason ye these things in your hearts?"

9. Whether is it easier to say to the sick of the palsy, Thy sins be forgiven thee; or to say, Arise, and take up thy bed, and walk?

10. But that ye may know that the Son of man hath power on earth to forgive sins, (he saith to the sick of the palsy,)

11. I say unto thee, Arise, and take up thy bed, and go thy way into thine house.

12. And immediately he arose, took up the bed, and went forth before them all; insomuch that they were all amazed, and glorified God, saying, "We never saw it on this fashion."

The Catholics confess their sin to a man called father, don't they? Once again, the Catholics are the fourth beast. He tells them how many hail Mary's to say, whatever that means. Do you not know that in football they have a pass called the Hail Mary Pass? What about hail Caesar or hail Hitler, sounds familiar?

Notice now that there is nothing about Hail Jesus which makes them the Anti-Christ. Everything in the Catholic organization is about Mary and not the Savior Jesus. I'm a little picky about the Lord when in Ephesians 3:15 states that the whole heaven and the earth is named after Jesus Christ. Now that's puzzling because how many streets are named after Jesus Christ?

You have a Main street, a Washington street, a Madison street and how about a Jefferson street in about every city but not one street named after Jesus Christ. FYI. Anti-Christ.

2 Thessalonians

1　Now we beseech you, brethren, by the coming of our Lord Jesus Christ, and by our gathering together unto him,

2　That ye be not soon shaken in mind, or be troubled, neither by spirit, nor by word, nor by letter as from us, as that the day of Christ is at hand.

3　Let no man deceive you by any means: for that day shall not come, except there come a falling away first, and that man of sin be revealed, the son of perdition;

4　Who opposeth and exalteth himself above all that is called God, or that is worshipped; so that he as God sitteth in the temple of God, shewing himself that he is God.

5　Remember ye not, that, when I was yet with you, I told you these things?

6　And now ye know what withholdeth that he might be revealed in his time.

59

7   For the mystery of iniquity doth already work: only he who now letteth will let, until he be taken out of the way.

8   And then shall that Wicked be revealed, whom the Lord shall consume with the spirit of his mouth, and shall destroy with the brightness of his coming:

9   Even him, whose coming is after the working of Satan with all power and signs and lying wonders,

10 And with all deceivableness of unrighteousness in them that perish; because they received not the love of the truth, that they might be saved.

11 And for this cause God shall send them strong delusion, that they should believe a lie:

12 That they all might be damned who believed not the truth, but had pleasure in unrighteousness.

The Pope is like a Rock Star because young people faint, they cry and cheer him on like he's Elvis or Michael Jackson. Did you know there's about 1.4 billion Catholics? Man, that's a lot of "Beast".

The Pope lives around Seven Mountains like what is prophecied in Revelation and also the Mascot of colors are mentioned as well.

Revelation 17

1   And there came one of the seven angels which had the seven vials, and talked with me, saying unto me, "Come hither"; I will shew unto thee the judgment of the great whore that sitteth upon many waters:

2   With whom the kings of the earth have committed fornication, and the inhabitants of the earth have been made drunk with the wine of her fornication.

3   So, he carried me away in the spirit into the wilderness: and I saw a woman sit upon a scarlet-coloured beast, full of names of blasphemy, having seven heads and ten horns. (What are the colors of Rome?)

4   And the woman was arrayed in purple and scarlet colour, and decked with gold and precious stones and pearls, having a golden cup in her hand full of abominations and filthiness of her fornication: (What are the colors of Rome?

5   And upon her forehead was a name written, Mystery, Babylon The Great, The Mother Of Harlots And Abominations Of The Earth.

6   And I saw the woman drunken with the blood of the saints, and with the blood of the martyrs of Jesus: and when I saw her, I wondered with great admiration.

7   And the angel said unto me, "Wherefore didst thou marvel? I will tell thee the mystery of the woman, and of the beast that carrieth her, which hath the seven heads and ten horns."

8   The beast that thou sawest was, and is not; and shall ascend out of the bottomless pit, and go into perdition: and they that dwell on the earth shall wonder, whose names were not written in the book of life from the foundation of the world, when they behold the beast that was, and is not, and yet is.

9   And here is the mind which hath wisdom. The seven heads are seven mountains, on which the woman sitteth.

10 And there are seven kings: five are fallen, and one is, and the other is not yet come; and when he cometh, he must continue a short space.

11 And the beast that was, and is not, even he is the eighth, and is of the seven, and goeth into perdition.

12 And the ten horns which thou sawest are ten kings, which have received no kingdom as yet; but receive power as kings one hour with the beast.

13 These have one mind, and shall give their power and strength unto the beast.

14 These shall make war with the Lamb, and the Lamb shall overcome them: for he is Lord of lords, and King of kings: and they that are with him are called, and chosen, and faithful.

15 And he saith unto me, "The waters which thou sawest, where the whore sitteth, are peoples, and multitudes, and nations, and tongues." (Today there are approximately 1.4 billion Catholics but not to say that also the rest of the world that follows their belief or worships the Calendar)

16 And the ten horns which thou sawest upon the beast, these shall hate the whore, and shall make her desolate and naked, and shall eat her flesh, and burn her with fire.

17 For God hath put in their hearts to fulfil his will, and to agree, and give their kingdom unto the beast, until the words of God shall be fulfilled.

18 And the woman which thou sawest is that great city, which reigneth over the kings of the earth.

The woman is the Catholic Organization.

Doesn't this sound just like Daniel chapter 7?

God is going to deceive you, and the devil is deceiving, so how can you stand? You are destined. This is how Rome operates, to study more about being in this life than knowing about God. Remember, they will change God's "times and laws."

Love not the world, neither the things that are in the world. If any man love the world, the love of the father is not in him. For all that is in the world, the lust of the flesh, and the lust of the eyes, and the pride of life, is not of the father, but is of the world. And the world passeth away, and the lust thereof: but he that doeth the will of God abideth forever. (1 John 2:15–17)

We will die one day with all of our lusts and pride of life. You know, the greed of this life is like "I want this car," "I want this house," or

"I want this job" but all for the wrong reasons. This life has become covetous and selfish, and I fell into this type of life myself because I thought, if the whites have it, I want it too. When I was a little boy, I started stealing because the white children had what I didn't have.

When you follow Rome, you'll get the mark of the Beast (666). Also, the influence of Rome is felt around the world every day, and the world is clueless that they are a part of prophecy and will be destroyed when Jesus comes. Have you ever asked yourself why do we need to know the Roman numerals in America, or why at the bottom of old movies in the credits are the dates in Roman numerals? Even some clocks still have the Roman numerals in 2021. I was a good street wrestler and also wrestled in the Marines for my unit, and that type of wrestling was called Greco-Roman wrestling.

THE INFLUENCE OF ROME UPON THE WORLD TODAY

Why is the White House called by that name and not the People's House or the President's Mansion? You have the governors' mansions, don't you? Why does America have governors as Rome did? Why does America have senators like the infamous Roman Senators who assassinated their ruler, Julius Caesar? Why is Capitol Hill in Washington named after one of Rome's infamous Seven Hills, mentioned in the book of Revelation?

Consider the opening of Revelation chapter 17: "And there came one of the seven angels which had the seven vials, and talked with me, saying unto me, Come hither; I will shew unto thee the judgment of the great whore that sitteth upon many waters" (vs. 1) Why this term? Read verse 2: "With whom the kings of the earth have committed fornication, and the inhabitants of the earth have been made drunk with the wine of her fornication." This is how you receive the mark of the Beast, by association with Rome and the pope. This is "spiritual fornication" by kings who have accepted Rome's times and laws by obeying the pagan holidays on the Julian calendar basically established in the year 666. Everyone who does those things on the calendar will receive the mark of the Beast.

Daniel 7:25 warned of those who would think to change the times and the laws. The Julian calendar basically started in the year 666, and Julius Caesar adopted it and updated it to suit their pagan holidays, starting with "Easter" and dealing with the sun, moon, and stars. Every country comes through Rome. And who is the spiritual leader of Rome? The pope.

Revelation 17:3–4 continues: "So he carried me away in the spirit into the wilderness: and I saw a woman sit upon a scarlet-coloured beast, full of names of blasphemy, having seven heads and ten horns. And the woman was arrayed in purple and scarlet colour, and decked with gold and precious stones and pearls, having a golden cup in her hand full of abominations and filthiness of her fornication." Note here the colors of Rome. And more: the pope rides in a gold chariot, and they take the cup during their communion.

By contrast, Jesus rides an ass colt. Before Jesus's triumphal entry into Jerusalem, the disciples brought the ass, and the colt, and put on them their clothes, and they set him thereon. And a very great multitude spread their garments in the way; others cut down branches from the trees, and strawed them in the way. And the multitudes that went before, and that followed, cried, saying, "Hosanna to the son of David: Blessed is he that cometh in the name of the Lord; Hosanna in the highest" (Matthew 21:7–9).

Whenever you welcome the pope to your country, you commit spiritual fornication. Please remember now, that Rome crucified Jesus Christ and the apostles and haven't been brought to court for their crimes, and God has a "vendetta" against them. Why? Because there is no statute of limitations for murdering innocent men who committed no crimes. "Behold, he cometh with clouds; and every eye shall see him, and they also which pierced him: and all kindreds of the earth shall wail because of him. Even so, Amen" (Revelation 1:7).

John 19:33–34 says, "But when they came to Jesus, and saw that he was dead already, they brake not his legs: but one of the soldiers with a spear pierced his side, and forthwith came there out blood and water."

This soldier represents Rome and their laws as to how they treat those who are dead already from being crucified.

I beheld till the thrones were cast down, and the Ancient of days did sit, whose garment was white as snow, and the hair of his head like the pure wool: his throne was like the fiery flame, and his wheels as burning fire. A fiery stream issued and came forth from before him: thousand thousands ministered unto him, and ten thousand times ten thousand stood before him: the judgment was set, and the books were opened.

I beheld then because of the voice of the great words which the horn spake: I beheld even till the beast was slain, and his body destroyed, and given to the burning flame. As concerning the rest of the beasts, they had their dominion taken away: yet their lives were prolonged for a season and time.

I saw in the night visions, and, behold, one like the Son of man came with the clouds of heaven, and came to the Ancient of days, and they brought him near before him. And there was given him dominion, and glory, and a kingdom, that all people, nations, and languages, should serve him: his dominion is an everlasting dominion, which shall not pass away, and his kingdom that which shall not be destroyed. (Daniel 7:9–14)

Back in Revelation 17:5–6, we read, "And upon her forehead was a name written, MYSTERY, BABYLON THE GREAT, THE MOTHER Of HARLOTS AND ABOMINATIONS Of THE EARTH. And I saw the woman drunken with the blood of the saints, and with the blood of the martyrs of Jesus: and when I saw her, I wondered with great admiration." Who crucified Jesus and killed the rest of the apostles? Who gave pagan names to the days of the week and the months of the year? Rome.

Rome has a murderous history and is full of mythology (fables) about gods and goddesses. The legend is that Romulus and Remus were two brothers, and they were suckled by a she wolf. (Who would want to believe that they come from something so devilish as that? But Rome must embellish this legend.) Rome started about 750 BCE, and the physical reign lasted to about 1400 AD. But the "mental reign" lasts to this day in 2021.

They "stamped the residue with their feet." They conquered, they stole, they pillaged, they raped, and they molested, and popes killed popes, and they assassinated each other, and you want to believe in them?

Go ahead, and get that mark of the Beast.

Revelation 17:7: "And the angel said unto me, Wherefore didst thou marvel? I will tell thee the mystery of the woman, and of the beast that carrieth her, which hath the seven heads and ten horns"—which stand for power and authority. Men name things after a woman—naming their car "Rosetta," for example. Remember that Jesus Christ's wife's name is the Church, which is a woman, but in this case in the book of Revelation, this woman is devilish. Just making comparisons.

YOUR DESTINY

"The beast that thou sawest was, and is not; and shall ascend out of the bottomless pit, and go into perdition: and they that dwell on the earth shall wonder, whose names were not written in the book of life from the foundation of the world, when they behold the beast that was, and is not, and yet is" (Revelation 17:8).

The Almighty God already knows if you are going to heaven or hell, but you don't know it. Isn't it something that there are people who are destined to hell, and they are at home watching TV or driving to the beach or on a cruise ship and don't know that they are already in hell?

SEVEN MOUNTAINS

Going on in Revelation 17, verse 9 reads, "And here is the mind which hath wisdom. The seven heads are seven mountains, on which the woman sitteth." Spiritually speaking, when God said, "I've been married to a backsliding Israel," Israel in this sense is a woman. So, in this case about the whore and where the woman sits, He is talking about a place in Rome called Vatican City where the pope sits amid seven hills.

The seven hills of Rome, according to Britannica, are Palatine Hill, Capitoline Hill (where does the White House sit?), Quirinal Hill, Viminal Hill, Esquiline Hill, Caelian Hill, and Aventine Hill. Why is the Senate named after the "Senate" that stabbed and killed Julius Caesar which was one of the horns plucked off according to Daniel? Why do we have governors just as Rome had governors during the crucifixion of Jesus? Why do the buildings on Capitol Hill look like they came from Rome?

Why is America so closely similar to Rome? Because George Washington was a Roman. He took this country by force (he stamped the residue, the Indians, with his feet) just as Rome did to the rest of the world before him, and then England tried to take America from Washington by doing the same. Why do I say that George Washington was a Roman? Because England at one time was called Roman Britannica. Rome warred over Britain about from 43 to 84 CE. So, the same ideals of Rome are in America too, which is the spreading of the mark of the Beast.

This world is "living prophecy," and they don't even know it. The world is just living, accepting life at face value, not knowing that someone wants to keep them that way—blind—and that makes them destined for hell.

Then came his disciples, and said unto him, "Knowest thou that the Pharisees were offended, after they heard this saying?"

But he answered and said, "Every plant, which my heavenly father hath not planted, shall be rooted up. Let them alone: they be blind leaders of the blind. And if the blind lead the blind, both shall fall into the ditch." (Matthew 15:12–14)

THE FOURTH BEAST'S "LAWS"

Rome crucified the Son of God, and you think that God is going to just let that go? If you believe in the influences or the ideals of Rome, God is coming after you too.

When the morning was come, all the chief priests and elders of the people took counsel against Jesus to put him to death: and when they had bound him, they led him away, and delivered him to Pontius Pilate the governor.

Then Judas, which had betrayed him, when he saw that he was condemned, repented himself, and brought again the thirty pieces of silver to the chief priests and elders, saying, "I have sinned in that I have betrayed the innocent blood."

And they said, "What is that to us? See thou to that."

And he cast down the pieces of silver in the temple, and departed, and went and hanged himself.

And the chief priests took the silver pieces, and said, "It is not lawful to put them into the treasury, because it is the price of blood." And they took counsel, and bought with them the potter's field, to bury strangers in. Wherefore that field was called, The field of blood, unto this day. Then was fulfilled that which was spoken by Jeremy [Jeremiah] the prophet, saying, "And they took the thirty pieces of silver, the price of him that was valued, whom they of the children of Israel did value

[Just like at this time in history, prophecies were being fulfilled, and the Jews and Romans had no clue]; and gave them for the potter's field, as the Lord appointed me."

And Jesus stood before the governor: and the governor asked him, saying, "Art thou the King of the Jews?" And Jesus said unto him, "Thou sayest."

And when he was accused of the chief priests and elders, he answered nothing. Then said Pilate unto him, "Hearest thou not how many things they witness against thee?" And he answered him to never a word; insomuch that the governor marvelled greatly.

Now at that feast the governor was wont to release unto the people a prisoner, whom they would. And they had then a notable prisoner, called Barabbas. Therefore, when they were gathered together, Pilate said unto them, "Whom will ye that I release unto you? Barabbas, or Jesus which is called Christ?" For he knew that for envy they had delivered him.

When he was set down on the judgment seat, his wife sent unto him, saying, "Have thou nothing to do with that just man: for I have suffered many things this day in a dream because of him."

But the chief priests and elders persuaded the multitude that they should ask Barabbas, and destroy Jesus.

The governor answered and said unto them, "Whether of the twain will ye that I release unto you?" They said, "Barabbas."

Pilate saith unto them, "What shall I do then with Jesus which is called Christ?" They all say unto him, "Let him be crucified."

And the governor said, "Why, what evil hath he done?" But they cried out the more, saying, "Let him be crucified."

When Pilate saw that he could prevail nothing, but that rather a tumult was made, he took water, and washed his hands before the multitude, saying, "I am innocent of the blood of this just person: see ye to it." [Roman law.]

Then answered all the people, and said, "His blood be on us, and on our children." [No truer words have ever been spoken.]

Then released he Barabbas unto them: and when he had scourged Jesus, he delivered him to be crucified. (Matthew 27:1–26)

"His blood be upon our children." Rome destroyed Israel, and so did other nations over the two- thousand-year period. Hitler killed close to six million during the Holocaust, and even to this very day they and their synagogues are bombed by the Palestinians. Check out this scripture:

And as they led him away, they laid hold upon one Simon, a Cyrenian, coming out of the country, and on him they laid the cross, that he might bear it after Jesus. And there followed him a great company of people, and of women, which also bewailed and lamented him. But Jesus turning unto them said, "Daughters of Jerusalem, weep not for me, but weep for yourselves, and for your children. [Someone has to pay for killing a sinless and innocent man. No one has ever been brought to trial for the death of Jesus Christ, the Son of God.] For, behold, the days are coming, in the which they shall say, Blessed are the barren, and the wombs that never bare, and the paps which never gave suck. [Wars and rumors of wars.] Then shall they begin to say to the mountains, fall on us; and to the hills, Cover us."

For if they do these things in a green tree, what shall be done in the dry? (Luke 23:26–31)

Wow—Roman laws. This was the justice system of the Roman Empire. Daniel 7:25 says of the fourth beast, "He shall speak great words against the most High, and shall wear out the saints of the most High, and think to change times and laws: and they shall be given into his hand until a time and times and the dividing of time."

Once again, Rome killed Jesus, the apostles, and the disciples. Rome is "white." Rome has white marble statues and buildings.

- Rome killed men, women and children.

- Rome "molested" men, women and children.

- Rome impregnated women of many cultures.

- Rome imposed their pagan religious beliefs upon man.

Is a "white lie" that different from a "black lie"? If a white cat crosses the street, then you can cross the street but if a black cat crosses the street, you have to turn and go back another way (fables)?

Halloween is a pagan holiday that deals with death. That's why you have ghosts and Frankenstein, skulls and the like, as well as black cats. The question is, Why not white cats? Who told a bunch of priest/monks to go and live together and a bunch of nuns to go and live together for so-called spiritual reasons? There is no such teaching in the Bible.

Today, in 2021, Roman Catholic priests are being convicted of molesting boys. These next scriptures are from the book of Romans—not written for the Roman Catholics but for the church of Christ in Rome, those who were converted from the Romans lifestyle during the times of the apostle Paul. In fact, this book is against the Roman Catholics. In the very beginning Paul hits a nerve in the culture of Rome dealing with homosexuals lesbians. No one has the right to do "Hate Crimes" against these people because we all have sin but if I have to repent of my sins so should they.

To all that be in Rome, beloved of God, called to be saints: Grace to you and peace from God our father, and the Lord Jesus Christ.

First, I thank my God through Jesus Christ for you all, that your faith is spoken of throughout the whole world. For God is my witness, whom I serve with my spirit in the gospel of his Son, that without ceasing I make mention of you always in my prayers; 10Making request, if by any means now at length I might have a prosperous journey by the will of God to come unto you.

For I long to see you, that I may impart unto you some spiritual gift, to the end ye may be established; that is, that I may be comforted together with you by the mutual faith both of you and me. Now I would not have you ignorant, brethren, that oftentimes I purposed to come unto you, (but was let hitherto,) that I might have some fruit among you also, even as among other Gentiles.

I am debtor both to the Greeks, and to the Barbarians; both to the wise, and to the unwise [Paul's perils in travels]. So, as much as in me is, I am ready to preach the gospel to you that are at Rome also.

For I am not ashamed of the gospel of Christ: for it is the power of God unto salvation to every one that believeth; to the Jew first, and also to the Greek. For therein is the righteousness of God revealed from faith to faith: as it is written, The just shall live by faith.

For the wrath of God is revealed from heaven against all ungodliness and unrighteousness of men, who hold the truth in unrighteousness [plagues: Covids, influenzas, AIDS, measles, chickenpox, flus, cancers of all kinds, sicknesses, diseases, and the likes; hurricanes, earthquakes, floods, tornados, tsunamis, famines, and the like]; because that which may be known of God is manifest in them; for God hath shewed it unto them. For the invisible things of him from the creation of the world are clearly seen, being understood by the things that are made, even his eternal power and Godhead; so that they are without excuse:

Because that, when they knew God, they glorified him not as God, neither were thankful; but became vain in their imaginations, and their foolish heart was darkened. Professing themselves to be wise, they became fools, and changed the glory of the uncorruptible God into an image made like to corruptible man, and to birds, and four-footed beasts, and creeping things [idolatry].

Wherefore God also gave them up to uncleanness through the lusts of their own hearts, to dishonour their own bodies between themselves: who changed the truth of God into a lie, and worshipped and served the creature more than the Creator, who is blessed forever. Amen.

For this cause God gave them up unto vile affections: for even their women did change the natural use into that which is against nature [lesbianism]: and likewise, also the men, leaving the natural use of the woman, burned in their lust one toward another; men with men working that which is unseemly, and receiving in themselves that recompence of their error which was meet.

And even as they did not like to retain God in their knowledge, God gave them over to a reprobate mind, to do those things which are not convenient; being filled with all unrighteousness, fornication, wickedness, covetousness, maliciousness; full of envy, murder, debate, deceit, malignity; whisperers, backbiters, haters of God, despiteful, proud, boasters, inventors of evil things, disobedient to parents, without understanding, covenant breakers, without natural affection, implacable, unmerciful: who knowing the judgment of God, that they which commit such things are worthy of death, not only do the same, but have pleasure in them that do ["I just want to see what they are doing"]. (Romans 1:7–32)

John 8

1   Jesus went unto the mount of Olives.

2   And early in the morning he came again into the temple, and all the people came unto him; and he sat down, and taught them.

4   And the scribes and Pharisees brought unto him a woman taken in adultery; and when they had set her in the midst,

4   They say unto him, Master, this woman was taken in adultery, in the very act.

5   Now Moses in the law commanded us, that such should be stoned: but what sayest thou?

6   This they said, tempting him, that they might have to accuse him. But Jesus stooped down, and with his finger wrote on the ground, as though he heard them not.

7   So, when they continued asking him, he lifted up himself, and said unto them, He that is without sin among you, let him first cast a stone at her.

8   And again, he stooped down, and wrote on the ground.

9   And they which heard it, being convicted by their own conscience, went out one by one, beginning at the eldest, even unto the last: and Jesus was left alone, and the woman standing in the midst.

10   When Jesus had lifted up himself, and saw none but the woman, he said unto her, "Woman, where are those thine accusers? hath no man condemned thee?"

11   She said, No man, Lord. And Jesus said unto her, "Neither do I condemn thee: go, and sin no more."

1 John

Chapter 3

15 Whosoever hateth his brother is a murderer: and ye know that no murderer hath eternal life abiding in him.

We don't actually have to physically harm someone we don't like for example wait outside of a Gay Club and do a drive-by and kill someone because the hate you had before the actual act makes you a murderer. Simply stating that just to hate someone because of their color you are a murderer in the eyes of God and no murderer as eternal life in them according to 1 John 3:1-15.

As for homosexuals, they have reaped many consequences, starting with the AIDS virus. Instead of changing their ways, they are given condoms and TV commercials to promote homosexuality. This also may pervert a young boy or girl to these "devilish ways" and corrupt their feeble minds. This is now the direction of the world.

It reminds me of this historical event, looking back on sin:

And there came two angels to Sodom at even; and Lot sat in the gate of Sodom: and Lot seeing them rose up to meet them; and he bowed himself with his face toward the ground; and he said, "Behold now, my lords, turn in, I pray you, into your servant's house, and tarry all night, and wash your feet, and ye shall rise up early, and go on your ways."

And they said, "Nay; but we will abide in the street all night."

And he pressed upon them greatly; and they turned in unto him, and entered into his house; and he made them a feast, and did bake unleavened bread, and they did eat.

4But before they lay down, the men of the city, even the men of Sodom, compassed the house round, both old and young, all the people from every quarter:

5And they called unto Lot, and said unto him, "Where are the men which came in to thee this night? Bring them out unto us, that we may know them." (To have sex with the two MEN angels).

And Lot went out at the door unto them, and shut the door after him, and said, "I pray you, brethren, do not so wickedly. Behold now, I have two daughters which have not known man; let me, I pray you, bring them out unto you, and do ye to them as is good in your eyes: only unto these men do nothing; for therefore came they under the shadow of my roof." [The people of Sodom and Gomorrah didn't want Lot's two daughters they wanted the two men, who were angels from God.]

And they said, "Stand back." And they said again, "This one fellow came in to sojourn, and he will need be a judge: now will we deal worse with thee, than with them." And they pressed sore upon the man, even Lot, and came near to break the door.

But the men put forth their hand, and pulled Lot into the house to them, and shut to the door. And they smote the men that were at the door of the house with blindness, both small and great: so that they wearied themselves to find the door.

And the men said unto Lot, "Hast thou here any besides? Son in law, and thy sons, and thy daughters, and whatsoever thou hast in the city, bring them out of this place: for we will destroy this place, because the cry of them is waxen great before the face of the LORD; and the LORD hath sent us to destroy it."

And Lot went out, and spake unto his sons in law, which married his daughters, and said, "Up, get you out of this place; for the LORD will destroy this city." But he seemed as one that mocked unto his sons in law. [They loved Sodom more than God, and so Lot's sons-in-law paid with their souls.]

And when the morning arose, then the angels hastened Lot, saying, "Arise, take thy wife, and thy two daughters, which are here; lest thou be consumed in the iniquity of the city."

And while he lingered, the men laid hold upon his hand, and upon the hand of his wife, and upon the hand of his two daughters; the LORD being merciful unto him: and they brought him forth, and set him without the city. And it came to pass, when they had brought them forth abroad, that he said, "Escape for thy life; look not behind thee, neither stay thou in all the plain; escape to the mountain, lest thou be consumed." (Genesis 19:1–17)

Romans 1:32 says, "Who knowing the judgment of God, that they which commit such things are worthy of death, not only do the same, but have pleasure in them that do them." With that, now back to the story of Lot:

And Lot said unto them, "Oh, not so, my LORD: behold now, thy servant hath found grace in thy sight, and thou hast magnified thy mercy, which thou hast shewed unto me in saving my life; and I cannot escape to the mountain, lest some evil take me, and I die: behold now, this city is near to flee unto, and it is a little one: Oh, let me escape thither, (is it not a little one?) and my soul shall live."

And he said unto him, "See, I have accepted thee concerning this thing also, that I will not overthrow this city, for the which thou hast spoken. Haste thee, escape thither; for I cannot do anything till thou become thither." Therefore, the name of the city was called Zoar.

The sun was risen upon the earth when Lot entered into Zoar. Then the LORD rained upon Sodom and upon Gomorrah brimstone and fire from the LORD out of heaven; and he overthrew those cities, and all the plain, and all the inhabitants of the cities, and that which grew upon the ground. But his wife looked back from behind him, and she became a pillar of salt. (Genesis 19:18–26)

In verse 17 the angels tell them not to look back on sin. To look back on the sins of Sodom and Gomorrah was death.

Rome literally and figuratively changed the landscape of the world. Every culture has done this, but Rome is in the forefront because God says they are. The fourth Beast laws are very simple, and they are anything against the laws of God. The key is that you would have to study the Word of God to know the Beast. Now that's the problem to have to study about yourself because the Bible is called the "Book of Life." No one wants to study about themselves—you know, sin.

Daniel 7:25 says, "And he shall speak great words against the most High, and shall wear out the saints of the most High, and think to change times and laws: and they shall be given into his hand until a time and times and the dividing of time" (until Jesus comes back). Let's see how this works because this is an inherited mental state from the fourth beast: The whites had a drinking fountain, and the blacks had a drinking fountain, the whites could come in the front door, but the Blacks had to come in the back door. The whites could sit in the front of the bus but the blacks had to sit in the back of the bus. During court proceedings the blacks had to sit in the balconies while the whites sat before the judge on the main floor. Now today to get a balcony seat you have to be rich. Go figure!

Some four thousand years ago the Lord taught his people this: "Thou shalt not avenge, nor bear any grudge against the children of thy people, but thou shalt love thy neighbor as thyself: I am the LORD" (Leviticus 19:18). Then in the New Testament:

Master, which is the great commandment in the law? Jesus said unto him, "Thou shalt love the Lord thy God with all thy heart, and with all thy soul, and with all thy mind. This is the first and great commandment. And the second is like unto it, Thou shalt love thy neighbour as thyself." On these two commandments hang all the law and the prophets. (Matthew 22:36-40)

I can enter through the front door of eateries, I can sit in the front seat of a bus, I can drink from any water fountain and the like. "You can't get to heaven without loving me!" Jesus Christ applies this commandment to the whole world, and it's not a "color scheme" that allows racism to discriminate.

But the fourth beast will kill, rape, inject their ideals into that culture, take over your lands, burn crosses in your yard, put you in slavery, lynch you or crucify you, not allow you to have credit or else give you credit at a higher percentage, won't allow you to vote, and the like. While I was in the Marines, I was discriminated against as well as other |African Americans who put their lives on the line for America.

The fourth beast will do this because he's the "greatest beast"; he has stamped the residue (conquered lands) with his feet. The fourth Beast will implement laws against The Almighty God and even act like The Almighty God.

Again, the devil taketh him up into an exceeding high mountain, and sheweth him all the kingdoms of the world, and the glory of them; and saith unto him, All these things will I give thee, if thou wilt fall down and worship me. [So, in order for you to "stamp" the residue with your feet, you will have to be worshiping the devil.]

Then saith Jesus unto him, Get thee hence, Satan: for it is written, Thou shalt worship the Lord thy God, and him only shalt thou serve. (Matthew 4:8–10)

The Supremacy of the fourth beast for a nation to do this, people would have to hate their neighbors.

In this the children of God are manifest, and the children of the devil: whosoever doeth not righteousness is not of God, neither he that loveth not his brother. [Brother in this sense embraces the world.]

For this is the message that ye heard from the beginning, that we should love one another. Not as Cain, who was of that wicked one, and slew his brother. And wherefore slew he him? Because his own works were evil, and his brother's righteous. Marvel not, my brethren, if the world hate you. We know that we have passed from death unto life, because we love the brethren. He that loveth not his brother abideth in death. Whosoever hateth his brother is a murderer: and ye know that no murderer hath eternal life abiding in him. (1 John 3:10–14)

When an apostle would go into a city, he was there to convert first Jews and then Gentiles (the world, or anyone who wasn't a Jew).

These twelve Jesus sent forth, and commanded them, saying, "Go not into the way of the Gentiles, and into any city of the Samaritans enter ye not: but go rather to the lost sheep of the house of Israel. And as ye go, preach, saying, The kingdom of heaven is at hand." (Matthew 10:5–7)

And when they opposed themselves, and blasphemed, he shook his raiment, and said unto them, "Your blood be upon your own heads; I am clean: from henceforth I will go unto the Gentiles." (Acts 18:6)

This is when the Gentiles were converted to Christ and became "spiritual brothers in Christ." If Paul was able to convert both of them by teaching them first about Jesus Christ and then baptizing them in the idolatrous world of that time, they would become "spiritual brothers"—neighbors. If you tried to leave an idolatrous world back then, they would kill you—and what about some communist nations today in 2021? They would kill you if you tried to leave their country.

ETHIOPIAN EUNUCH SAVED BY DOING WHAT?

And the angel of the Lord spake unto Philip, saying, "Arise, and go toward the south unto the way that goeth down from Jerusalem unto Gaza, which is desert. And he arose and went: and, behold, a man of Ethiopia, an eunuch of great authority under Candace queen of the Ethiopians, who had the charge of all her treasure, and had come to Jerusalem for to worship, was returning, and sitting in his chariot read Esaias the prophet." Then the Spirit said unto Philip, "Go near, and join thyself to this chariot."

And Philip ran thither to him, and heard him read the prophet Esaias, and said, "Understandest thou what thou readest?"

And he said, "How can I, except some man should guide me?" And he desired Philip that he would come up and sit with him.

The place of the scripture which he read was this, He was led as a sheep to the slaughter; and like a lamb dumb before his shearer, so opened he not his mouth: in his humiliation his judgment was taken away: and who shall declare his generation? For his life is taken from the earth.

And the eunuch answered Philip, and said, "I pray thee, of whom speaketh the prophet this? of himself, or of some other man?" Then Philip opened his mouth, and began at the same scripture, and preached unto him Jesus.

And as they went on their way, they came unto a certain water: and the eunuch said, "See, here is water; what doth hinder me to be baptized?" And Philip said, "If thou believest with all thine heart, thou mayest." And he answered and said, "I believe that Jesus Christ is the Son of God." And he commanded the chariot to stand still: and they went down both into the water, both Philip and the eunuch; and he baptized him. [Not one word about "praying the sinner's prayer"; there is no such animal taught in the Scriptures.] And when they were come up out of the water, the Spirit of the Lord caught away Philip, that the eunuch saw him no more: and he went on his way rejoicing. (Acts 8:26–39)

Revelation 12:12 says, "Therefore rejoice, ye heavens, and ye that dwell in them. Woe to the inhabiters of the earth and of the sea! For the devil is come down unto you, having great wrath, because he knoweth that he hath but a short time." You do know that Satan is after you, whether young or old, big or small, rich or poor, right? I mean every day of your life the devil is after you. Satan can get you by accidents, fires, at your job, at night clubs, through domestic violence, fighting, drinking too much, shootings, the military, school shootings, being at the wrong place at the wrong time but the right time for the devil—and you may have been brought their by the devil himself—also by diseases: Covid-19, SARS, influenza, AIDS, cancers of all types, and other sicknesses.

"I was wondering why page 78 about the Ethiopian Eunuch was in that place and I believe it's because of the previous pages about conversions. Just leave it there.

There's so much in this mind that I just go off topic then I have to find my way back and even then, I'm like why did I say that.

I find that God is like that too. I try to write from the beginning to the end but in doing so there's the future and the past to put together to make this story. I don't know if I over think it with all of this running in my mind about life and death concerning the scriptures.

If you read the book of Revelations, you will find that God is like that too. He'll throw you into the future then back to the past then in the middle all in one scripture.

Remember now that this book is a dream or vision and do dreams make since? No.

Remember Joseph and his dreams that took some 20 years to come to pass to fulfill God's promises to Abraham and that his children who would be in slavery for four hundred years?

Now that's God at his best to keep the devil off his toes and to deliver a message to his believers who are destined and to keep out those who are not destined. That in time his believers will figure it out and be saved.

Even this very page we're talking about is about prophecy of the life and death of a man called Jesus. But no one knows that they're living in that time but Philip to save this Eunuch who's from Africa.

Just like today we live in the world of the fourth beast and receiving the Mark of the beast by doing those things on the calendar created by the beast.

No one in this world is the wiser but people like the Ethiopian Eunuch who wanted to learn the word of God in truth.

This world is about water cooler talk and nothing about God.

Amazing how the Almighty God worked this out before he created the world.

See how complicated this is?

It's a mindset like the FBI having to think like a mass murderer to catch him or her.

So, leave 78 where it is."

THE CHURCH

How do I start this? I will summarize from "the beginning":

In the beginning God made heaven and earth. God made the sun, the moon, and the stars of heaven, and He made the oceans, rivers, lakes, and seas. He made all types of animals on land and sea, and then He made Man and Woman to take care of what He had created.

God made the world for man. The first man was called Adam, and the first woman was called Eve, and like the animals they were to be fruitful and to multiply. Both man and woman had a job working in a place called the garden of Eden, and they were told that they could eat of every tree in the garden except of the Tree of Knowledge of Good and Evil" but if they did eat of it or touch it that they would surely die.

Adam and Eve were created as a grown man and woman with very little knowledge, something like that of a two-year-old baby. They had no learning or understanding. So, when given their first opportunity to obey this heavenly voice, they didn't understand death. So, in process of time—meaning we don't know how long; it could have been a year or hundreds of years before they disobeyed God when the woman, Eve, tricked by the serpent, became the first to eat of the Tree of the Knowledge of Good and Evil and then gave to her husband Adam to eat also.

Things began to change in the minds of Adam and Eve as they understood some of "the Knowledge of Good and Evil." The Almighty God found out and punished each of them. The serpent, because he instigated the sin of disobedience, was punished first. (God made him to crawl on his belly all the days of his life.) Eve was next in line to be punished, and God made her to obey her husband Adam in all things and decreed that she would bear children in sorrow. Which meant in part that her children would now die, and this "prophecy" was fulfilled during her lifetime because her first son, Cain, killed his brother Abel. Not only was this the "sorrow" part, but this act by Cain was the first murder upon earth.

I can relate to this because my mom lost her two oldest daughters before she died, and from the sorrow on her face, I could feel the pains. My mom almost died at her oldest daughter's funeral. They all lay side by side by side in the cemetery. Death.

Adam was punished last, and because he obeyed his wife and ate the forbidden fruit, he was to work by the sweat of his brow until he died. Death.

Adam and Eve were kicked out of the garden of Eden never to return, and they multiplied to fill the earth as well as sin and death. (Adam lived to be 930 years old in those days.) God became angry with man, and He repented that He had made man, so He found the most righteous man on the earth, and that was Noah. God told Noah that He was going to destroy humanity with a flood; by the waters he would drown everyone.

Noah had a family of eight, including his wife and three boys with their wives. The Lord instructed him to build an Ark of different materials with pitch and measurements to provide shelter for all of his family and two animals of every kind upon the face of the earth. Noah and his family prepared to build the Ark as God had told him, but the neighborhood mocked him for building a boat on dry ground and no water in sight.

And it came to pass, when men began to multiply on the face of the earth, and daughters were born unto them, that the sons of God saw the daughters of men that they were fair; and they took them wives of all which they chose. And the LORD said, "My spirit shall not always strive with man, for that he also is flesh: yet his days shall be an hundred and twenty years."

There were giants in the earth in those days; and also, after that, when the sons of God came in unto the daughters of men, and they bear children to them, the same became mighty men which were of old, men of renown.

And God saw that the wickedness of man was great in the earth, and that every imagination of the thoughts of his heart was only evil continually. And it repented the LORD that he had made man on the earth, and it grieved him at his heart. And the LORD said, "I will destroy man whom I have created from the face of the earth; both man, and beast, and the creeping thing, and the fowls of the air; for it repenteth me that I have made them." But Noah found grace in the eyes of the LORD.

These are the generations of Noah: Noah was a just man and perfect in his generations, and Noah walked with God. And Noah begat three sons, Shem, Ham, and Japheth.

The earth also was corrupt before God, and the earth was filled with violence. And God looked upon the earth, and behold, it was corrupt; for all flesh had corrupted his way upon the earth. And God said unto Noah, "The end of all flesh is come before me; for the earth is filled with violence through them; and, behold, I will destroy them with the earth. Make thee an ark of gopher wood; rooms shalt thou make in the ark, and shalt pitch it within and without with pitch. And this is the fashion which thou shalt make it of: The length of the ark shall be three hundred cubits, the breadth of it fifty cubits, and the height of it thirty cubits. A window shalt thou make to the ark, and in a cubit shalt thou finish it above; and the door of the ark shalt thou set in the side thereof; with lower, second, and third stories shalt thou make it. And, behold, I, even I, do bring a flood of waters upon the earth, to destroy all flesh, wherein is the breath of life, from under heaven; and every thing that is in the earth shall die. But with thee will I establish my covenant; and thou shalt come into the ark, thou, and thy sons, and thy wife, and thy sons' wives with thee. And of every living thing of all flesh, two of every sort shalt thou bring into the ark, to keep them alive with thee; they shall be male and female. Of fowls after their kind, and of cattle after their kind, of every creeping thing of the earth after his kind, two of every sort shall come unto thee, to keep them alive. And take thou unto thee of all food that is eaten, and thou shalt gather it to thee; and it shall be for food for thee, and for them."

Thus did Noah; according to all that God commanded him, so did he. (Genesis 6:1–22)

This how God works: He will find a few people throughout time to fulfil His will, regardless of how the world thinks.

Now, as the world continued to sin, God told Noah that it was time to load up the ark, and Noah did as commanded. Then the Lord flooded the world for forty days and nights until He decided that he had killed off all of mankind and the animals.

Noah and his family replenished the earth, and God made a promise not to kill humanity in this way ever again. Noah and his family died, but there came another man named Abram and his wife Sarai, and Abram found grace in the sight of the Lord, and God blessed Abram with earthly goods. Now, you may have earthly goods, but that alone doesn't mean anything. Why? Because God hasn't made a covenant with you like he did with Abram.

Abram was so righteous and such a believer in God that the Lord changed his name to Abraham, meaning "father of many nations," and Sarai's name to Sarah. God also made a covenant with Abraham through circumcision, and every male from eight days and older must be circumcised. Anyone who wasn't circumcised was kicked out of the camp of Abraham but mainly the "camp of God."

And when Abram was ninety years old and nine, the LORD appeared to Abram, and said unto him, "I am the Almighty God; walk before me, and be thou perfect. And I will make my covenant between me and thee, and will multiply thee exceedingly."

And Abram fell on his face: and God talked with him, saying, "As for me, behold, my covenant is with thee, and thou shalt be a father of many nations. Neither shall thy name any more be called Abram, but thy name shall be Abraham; for a father of many nations have I made thee. And I will make thee exceeding fruitful, and I will make nations of thee, and kings shall come out of thee. And I will establish my covenant between me and thee and thy seed after thee in their generations for an everlasting covenant, to be a God unto thee, and to thy seed after thee. And I will give unto thee, and to thy seed after thee, the land wherein thou art a stranger, all the land of Canaan, for an everlasting possession; and I will be their God [not Rome's, Egypt's, Asia's, Africa's, or all of Europe's God but only Abraham's and his children's God]."

And God said unto Abraham, "Thou shalt keep my covenant therefore, thou, and thy seed after thee in their generations. [The next verse is key to understanding the Old Testament's physical circumcision and the New Testament's spiritual circumcision.] This is my covenant, which ye shall keep, between me and you and thy seed after thee; Every man child among you shall be circumcised." (Genesis 17:1–10)

Circumcision has to do with being clean, pure, and righteous. If a man was not circumcised and he had sex with his wife, she could get an infection from her husband which could cause harm or deformity to the child. This is where you get the terms uncircumcised and Gentile, which meant anyone who wasn't a Jew. God had no covenant relations with them. Jesus Christ would also have to come through this pure lineage.

And ye shall circumcise the flesh of your foreskin; and it shall be a token of the covenant betwixt me and you. And he that is eight days old shall be circumcised among you, every man child in your generations, he that is born in the house, or bought with money of any stranger, which is not of thy seed. He that is born in thy house, and he that is bought with thy money, must needs be circumcised: and my covenant shall be in your flesh for an everlasting covenant. And the uncircumcised man child whose flesh of his foreskin is not circumcised, that soul shall be cut off from his people; he hath broken my covenant.

And God said unto Abraham, "As for Sarai thy wife, thou shalt not call her name Sarai, but Sarah shall her name be. And I will bless her, and give thee a son also of her: yea, I will bless her, and she shall be a mother of nations; kings of people shall be of her."

Then Abraham fell upon his face, and laughed, and said in his heart, "Shall a child be born unto him that is an hundred years old? And shall Sarah, that is ninety years old, bear?" And Abraham said unto God, "O that Ishmael might live before thee!"

And God said, "Sarah thy wife shall bear thee a son indeed; and thou shalt call his name Isaac: and I will establish my covenant with him for an everlasting covenant, and with his seed after him. And as for Ishmael, I have heard thee: Behold, I have blessed him, and will make him fruitful, and will multiply him exceedingly; twelve princes shall he beget, and I will make him a great nation. But my covenant will I establish with Isaac, which Sarah shall bear unto thee at this set time in the next year." And he left off talking with him, and God went up from Abraham.

And Abraham took Ishmael his son, and all that were born in his house, and all that were bought with his money, every male among the men of Abraham's house; and circumcised the flesh of their foreskin in the selfsame day, as God had said unto him. And Abraham was ninety years old and nine, when he was circumcised in the flesh of his foreskin. And Ishmael his son was thirteen years old, when he was circumcised in the flesh of his foreskin. In the selfsame day was Abraham circumcised, and Ishmael his son. And all the men of his house, born in the house, and bought with money of the stranger, were circumcised with him. (Genesis 17:11–27)

God also told Abraham that his children would be in slavery for four hundred years and that He would bring them out to this land of Canaan. But for this to happen, Abraham had to have children and he was in his nineties, and Sarah was barren and laughed at the fact that she was barren, so what a task. "And he said unto Abram, Know of a surety that thy seed shall be a stranger in a land that is not theirs, and shall serve them; and they shall afflict them four hundred years" (Genesis 15:13).

You know, I can vouch for Abraham how hard a task this might be. Most men today have problems being intimate with their wives in their late forties to early fifties, and Abraham was in his nineties, and the inheritance of Jesus Christ would come through him. Abraham was blessed to have had Isaac, and Isaac's son Jacob had twelve sons from two wives and two maids. Jacob's name was changed to "Israel" meaning "Prince." Jacob by having these twelve sons would be called the father of the twelve tribes of Israel.

Now these are the names of the tribes. From the north end to the coast of the way of Hethlon, as one goeth to Hamath, Hazarenan, the border of Damascus northward, to the coast of Hamath; for these are his sides east and west; a portion for Dan. And by the border of Dan, from the east side unto the west side, a portion for Asher. And by the border of Asher, from the east side even unto the west side, a portion for Naphtali. And by the border of Naphtali, from the east side unto the west side, a portion for Manasseh.

And by the border of Manasseh, from the east side unto the west side, a portion for Ephraim. [Manasseh and Ephraim were grafted in for land by being Joseph's sons.] And by the border of Ephraim, from the east side even unto the west side, a portion for Reuben. And by the border of Reuben, from the east side unto the west side, a portion for Judah ....

And over against the border of the priests the Levites shall have five and twenty thousand in length, and ten thousand in breadth: all the length shall be five and twenty thousand, and the breadth ten thousand ....

And by the border of Benjamin, from the east side unto the west side, Simeon shall have a portion. And by the border of Simeon, from the east side unto the west side, Issachar a portion. And by the border of Issachar, from the east side unto the west side, Zebulun a portion. And by the border of Zebulun, from the east side unto the west side, Gad a portion. And by the border of Gad, at the south side southward, the border shall be even from Tamar unto the waters of strife in Kadesh, and to the river toward the great sea. This is the land which ye shall divide by lot unto the tribes of Israel for inheritance, and these are their portions, saith the Lord God. (Ezekiel 48:1–7, 13, 24–29)

Notice that God chose Israel through Abraham to be His people instead of Rome, Egypt, Africa, Babylon, Asia, and the rest of Europe. This is key to understanding God and His worshipping concept in that He always had one people of believers. Truly this is very important to understanding the invisible God in how He taught Israel in worshipping Him, and if they varied, they were destroyed.

Now the rest of the world was lawless in that they established their own laws mostly by hierarchy. Those other nations worshiped many different gods of gold, silver, iron, brass, copper, and stone. Then they would have human sacrifices, even offering up their children. "And they built the high places of Baal, which are in the Valley of the Son of Hinnom, to cause their sons and their daughters to pass through the fire unto Molech, which I commanded them not, neither came it into My mind that they should do this abomination, to cause Judah to sin" (Jeremiah 32:35). So, to keep the children of Israel honest He never showed them His face so that they wouldn't make an image of Him; therefore, He is the invisible God of Israel.

Notice how prophecy works as we go along here, pertaining to how Israel and his children will be led to a distant land and then into slavery. Israel had a special son named Joseph, and Joseph was a "dreamer of dreams," and his dreams would become true. Now, Israel loved Joseph, but Israel's other sons were jealous of Joseph. "Now Israel loved Joseph more than all his children, because he was the son of his old age: and he made him a coat of many colours" (Genesis 37:3).

And Joseph dreamed a dream, and he told it his brethren: and they hated him yet the more. And he said unto them, "Hear, I pray you, this dream which I have dreamed: for, behold, we were binding sheaves in the field, and, lo, my sheaf arose, and also stood upright; and, behold, your sheaves stood round about, and made obeisance to my sheaf."

And his brethren said to him, "Shalt thou indeed reign over us? or shalt thou indeed have dominion over us?" And they hated him yet the more for his dreams, and for his words.

And he dreamed yet another dream, and told it his brethren, and said, "Behold, I have dreamed a dream more; and, behold, the sun and the moon and the eleven stars made obeisance to me."

And he told it to his father, and to his brethren: and his father rebuked him, and said unto him, "What is this dream that thou hast dreamed? Shall I and thy mother and thy brethren indeed come to bow down ourselves to thee to the earth?" And his brethren envied him; but his father observed the saying. (Genesis 37:5–11)

So, they conspired to get rid of Joseph because in one of Joseph's dream he interpreted that his brothers would bow to him. While in the fields with the herd, they seized Joseph and put him in a hole, but Joseph made so much noise that when some tradesmen came by, they sold him to them, and Joseph was taken into another country called Egypt.

Now the sons had to make up a lie as to how Joseph disappeared so they killed a young goat and put the blooishmad on a garment of Joseph and brought it to their father Israel, and he just cried.

And it came to pass, when Joseph was come unto his brethren, that they stript Joseph out of his coat, his coat of many colours that was on him; and they took him, and cast him into a pit: and the pit was empty, there was no water in it.

And they sat down to eat bread: and they lifted up their eyes and looked, and behold, a company of Ishmeelites came from Gilead with their camels bearing spicery and balm and myrrh, going to carry it down to Egypt.

And Judah said unto his brethren, "What profit is it if we slay our brother, and conceal his blood? Come, and let us sell him to the Ishmeelites, and let not our hand be upon him; for he is our brother and our flesh. And his brethren were content."

Then there passed by Midianites merchantmen; and they drew and lifted up Joseph out of the pit, and sold Joseph to the Ishmeelites for twenty pieces of silver: and they brought Joseph into Egypt.

And Reuben returned unto the pit; and, behold, Joseph was not in the pit; and he rent his clothes. And he returned unto his brethren, and said, "The child is not; and I, whither shall I go?" And they took Joseph's coat, and killed a kid of the goats, and dipped the coat in the blood; and they sent the coat of many colours, and they brought it to their father; and said, "This have we found: know now whether it be thy son's coat or no."

And he knew it, and said, "It is my son's coat; an evil beast hath devoured him; Joseph is without doubt rent in pieces."

And Jacob rent his clothes, and put sackcloth upon his loins, and mourned for his son many days. And all his sons and all his daughters rose up to comfort him; but he refused to be comforted; and he said, "For I will go down into the grave unto my son mourning." Thus, his father wept for him.

And the Midianites sold him into Egypt unto Potiphar, an officer of Pharaoh's, and captain of the guard. (Genesis 37:23–36)

In the process of time, Joseph prospered in the land and became very popular but never forgot his roots and the Lord.

Trust me, when everything is going well, there comes evil. Potiphar, the captain of the guard had put Joseph in charge of his possessions, but Potiphar's wife liked Joseph. So, she made many advancements toward Joseph, but he kept his faith in God not to be involved with his master's wife. In the end, she accused Joseph of making advancements, and Potiphar reluctantly had Joseph imprisoned. While Joseph was in prison, two men had dreams, and he interpreted the dreams that one of them would be executed and the other would be given back his old job with Pharaoh.

Joseph was right about the dreams, and it came to pass that Pharaoh had a dream and wanted to know what it meant, and the man who had been in prison remembered that Joseph interpreted his dream, so Joseph was called to interpret Pharaoh's dream. Joseph's interpretation was that there would be a famine in all the land and that they should store up grain for seven years. By this wisdom Joseph was truly gifted by God.

Now Israel was in need of food due to the famine, and he knew that Egypt had food, so Israel and his family left to go to Egypt. Once they were in Egypt, Joseph told Israel's sons that he was Joseph and how God had placed him in Egypt for that purpose, and they were very emotional and overwhelmed with joy.

In the course of time, both Israel and Joseph had died, and there was a new Pharaoh. The children of Israel multiplied in the land, and the Egyptians feared the children of Israel and they put them in bondage and made them slaves for four hundred years. This is a form of racism. The Jews were seeking a deliverer to bring them out of slavery during these four hundred years, and a child was born named Moses. Egypt heard of the foretelling of this deliverer, and so they killed all Jewish boys up to two years old, hoping to remove the deliverer.

Moses as a child mysteriously, by the mighty hand of God, escaped the sword of the Egyptians and was mistakenly taken into the Egyptian family of Pharaoh. Moses grew up as a young mighty Prince in Egypt, but it was found out that he truly wasn't an Egyptian, so Moses was booted out of the land into the wilderness.

This is key, in that Moses was of the tribe of Levi, one of the sons of Jacob. Once Israel was freed from slavery, God kept the tribe of Levi to be His only priests to minister to Him and for the people of Israel in the whole wide world. No one else—neither the other eleven tribes of Israel nor Rome, Asia, Egypt, Africa, Britain, Babylon, or Greece—could offer anything to God except the Levitical priesthood, and if anyone tried, they were killed.

Moses, being led in the wilderness by God for forty days, found a place called Midian, and there he raised his family and became a sheep herder. Moses never forgot the pains of Egypt and his people being in slavery, so after forty years in the land of Midian, he saw a burning bush on a mountain while he tended his sheep and went up to see the sight. There Moses encountered the almighty God on the mountain, and the Lord spoke to Moses from the burning bush and expressed His concerns about His people Israel. He announced that Moses was the deliverer to bring His people out of slavery by the hands of the Egyptians.

This has to be one of the most impressive images in the mind of Moses's life. Where he came from, in the land of Egypt, there were images of rocks and stones that didn't speak, hear, or walk. God knows how to get your attention, and if the fourth beast hasn't, you're already dead because unlike Moses this woke his living soul right out of the grave.

The Awakening

I say this because what I've learned from my sixty-two-year "walk of life" and the wisdom I've been blessed with has brought me from the spiritually dead to the spiritually living. I can see. Moses and his brother, Aaron, being led by the strict commandments of God, spoke to Pharaoh, saying that the invisible God wanted His people Israel to be freed from slavery so that they could worship Him in the wilderness. Pharaoh, full of pride, denied all of the commandments of this "invisible God" delivered by Moses (because Egyptians couldn't believe in anything they couldn't see). So, over a period of time God put seven plagues in Egypt, and on the seventh plague Pharaoh bowed down to Moses and God and let Israel go free with great wealth. Moses Returns to Egypt.

And the LORD said unto Moses, "See, I have made thee a god to Pharaoh: and Aaron thy brother shall be thy prophet. Thou shalt speak all that I command thee: and Aaron thy brother shall speak unto Pharaoh, that he sends the children of Israel out of his land. And I will harden Pharaoh's heart, and multiply my signs and my wonders in the land of Egypt. But Pharaoh shall not hearken unto you, that I may lay my hand upon Egypt, and bring forth mine armies, and my people the children of Israel, out of the land of Egypt by great judgments. And the Egyptians shall know that I am the LORD, when I stretch forth mine hand upon Egypt, and bring out the children of Israel from among them."

And Moses and Aaron did as the LORD commanded them, so did they. And Moses was fourscore years old [eighty years old], and Aaron fourscore and three years old, when they spake unto Pharaoh. (Exodus 7:1–7)

And afterward Moses and Aaron went in, and told Pharaoh, "Thus saith the LORD God of Israel, Let my people go, that they may hold a feast unto me in the wilderness." And Pharaoh said, "Who is the LORD, that I should obey his voice to let Israel go? I know not the LORD, neither will I let Israel go."

3And they said, "The God of the Hebrews hath met with us: let us go, we pray thee, three days' journey into the desert, and sacrifice unto the LORD our God; lest he fall upon us with pestilence, or with the sword."

And the king of Egypt said unto them, "Wherefore do ye, Moses and Aaron, let the people from their works? Get you unto your burdens." (Exodus 5:1–4)

THE TEN PLAGUES OF EGYPT

1. Water turned to blood

2. Frogs

3. Lice

4. Gnats

5. Diseased livestock

6. Boils

7. Hail

8. Locusts

9. Darkness

10. Killing all the firstborn males of Egypt. Remember what one of the Pharaohs had done some years earlier by killing the two-year-old male children of Israel in an effort to kill Moses to stop the deliverer.

The Jews didn't really know what to think of Moses, their deliverer, because at times they wanted to kill him. This attitude, this "caveman" mentality of bitterness, depression, and oppression due to being in bondage for four hundred years, took a toll on their lives. The Jews no doubt constructed some of the pyramids and sphinxes, which are forms of idolatry, so the Jews would take this mindset of stubbornness and rebellion with them when they were freed. You need to understand that the Lord hadn't spoken to the Jews in four hundred years and that there was no law of righteousness in the land, so the Jews were just as lawless as the Egyptians. The straw that broke Pharaoh's back was the tenth plague, which killed all the firstborn males in the whole land of Egypt, including Pharaoh's only son, the heir to the throne.

THE EXODUS

Exodus means mass departure or emigration. Keep in mind that the Word of God means something, and it has no meaning of idolatry.

As you read chapter 12 in the book of Exodus, you will see the first time that the Jews worshipped the Lord, and this type of worship carried on until Jesus established His kingdom, the church, in the New Testament. You will also find similarities in the Passover to Jesus Christ, in that under the Old Testament the Jews offered an animal sacrifice, which was a young male lamb. Under the New Testament, Jesus Christ was a human sacrifice at the young age of thirty-three and was called the Lamb of God. Jesus Christ during the Passover instituted the Lord's Supper and was crucified also during the Passover period.

And the LORD spake unto Moses and Aaron in the land of Egypt, saying, "This month shall be unto you the beginning of months: it shall be the first month of the year to you. Speak ye unto all the congregation of Israel, saying, in the tenth day of this month they shall take to them every man a lamb, according to the house of their fathers, a lamb for an house: and if the household be too little for the lamb, let him and his neighbour next unto his house take it according to the number of the souls; every man according to his eating shall make your count for the lamb. Your lamb shall be without blemish, a male of the first year: ye shall take it out from the sheep, or from the goats [Jesus was sinless, without blemish.]: and ye shall keep it up until the fourteenth day of the same month: and the whole assembly of the congregation of Israel shall kill it in the evening. And they shall take of the blood and strike it on the two side posts and on the upper door post of the houses, wherein they shall eat it. And they shall eat the flesh in that night, roast with fire, and unleavened bread; and with bitter herbs they shall eat it. Eat not of it raw, nor sodden at all with water, but roast with fire; his head with his legs, and with the purtenance thereof. And ye shall let nothing of it remain until the morning; and that which remaineth of it until the morning ye shall burn with fire. And thus shall ye eat it; with your loins girded, your shoes on your feet, and your staff in your hand; and ye shall eat it in haste: it is the LORD's Passover."

For I will pass through the land of Egypt this night, and will smite all the firstborn in the land of Egypt, both man and beast; and against all the gods of Egypt I will execute judgment: I am the LORD. (Exodus 12:1–12)

The Passover was not a joke; it was serious stuff. You had to be united on all fronts when partaking of the Passover, or you would be killed like the Egyptians. You must be ready to partake and righteous. Remember, during the Lord's Supper, one of the twelve apostles was a "devil" named Judas Iscariot, who betrayed the Lord and afterwards committed suicide.

Now when the even was come, he sat down with the twelve. And as they did eat, he said, "Verily I say unto you, that one of you shall betray me."

And they were exceeding sorrowful, and began every one of them to say unto him, "Lord, is it I?" And he answered and said, "He that dippeth his hand with me in the dish, the same shall betray me. The Son of man goeth as it is written of him: but woe unto that man by whom the Son of man is betrayed! It had been good for that man if he had not been born."

Then Judas, which betrayed him, answered and said," Master, is it I?" He said unto him, "Thou hast said."

And as they were eating, Jesus took bread, and blessed it, and brake it, and gave it to the disciples, and said, "Take, eat; this is my body." (Matthew 26:20–26)

And Judas Iscariot, one of the twelve, went unto the chief priests, to betray him unto them. And when they heard it, they were glad, and promised to give him money. And he sought how he might conveniently betray him. (Mark 14:10–11)

Judas Commits Suicide

When the morning was come, all the chief priests and elders of the people took counsel against Jesus to put him to death: and when they had bound him, they led him away, and delivered him to Pontius Pilate the governor.

Then Judas, which had betrayed him, when he saw that he was condemned, repented himself, and brought again the thirty pieces of silver to the chief priests and elders, saying, "I have sinned in that I have betrayed the innocent blood."

And they said, "What is that to us? See thou to that."

And he cast down the pieces of silver in the temple, and departed, and went and hanged himself.

And the chief priests took the silver pieces, and said, "It is not lawful for to put them into the treasury, because it is the price of blood." (Matthew 27:1–6)

And when he had given thanks, he brake it, and said, "Take, eat: this is my body, which is broken for you: this do in remembrance of me." After the same manner also he took the cup, when he had supped, saying, "This cup is the new testament in my blood: this do ye, as oft as ye drink it, in remembrance of me. For as often as ye eat this bread, and drink this cup, ye do shew the Lord's death till he come."

Wherefore whosoever shall eat this bread, and drink this cup of the Lord, unworthily, shall be guilty of the body and blood of the Lord. But let a man examine himself, and so let him eat of that bread, and drink of that cup. For he that eateth and drinketh unworthily, eateth and drinketh damnation to himself, not discerning the Lord's body. For this cause many are weak and sickly among you, and many sleep. (1 Corinthians 11:24–30)

(Sleep means they died for partaking in the Lord's Supper with sin on their souls.)

"Drinking from the Wrong Cup" of the Fourth Beast

For all nations have drunk of the wine of the wrath of her fornication, and the kings of the earth have committed fornication with her, and the merchants of the earth are waxed rich through the abundance of her delicacies.

And I heard another voice from heaven, saying, "Come out of her, my people, that ye be not partakers of her sins, and that ye receive not of her plagues. For her sins have reached unto heaven, and God hath remembered her iniquities. Reward her even as she rewarded you, and double unto her double according to her works: in the cup which she hath filled fill to her double. How much she hath glorified herself, and lived deliciously, so much torment and sorrow give her: for she saith in her heart, I sit a queen, and am no widow, and shall see no sorrow. Therefore, shall her plagues come in one day, death, and mourning, and famine; and she shall be utterly burned with fire: for strong is the Lord God who judgeth her."

And the kings of the earth, who have committed fornication and lived deliciously with her, shall bewail her, and lament for her, when they shall see the smoke of her burning. (Revelation 18:3–9)

Be careful who you drink with.

And there came one of the seven angels which had the seven vials, and talked with me, saying unto me, "Come hither; I will shew unto thee the judgment of the great whore that sitteth upon many waters: with whom the kings of the earth have committed fornication, and the inhabitants of the earth have been made drunk with the wine of her fornication."

So, he carried me away in the spirit into the wilderness: and I saw a woman sit upon a scarlet coloured beast, full of names of blasphemy, having seven heads and ten horns. And the woman was arrayed in purple and scarlet colour, and decked with gold and precious stones and pearls, having a golden cup in her hand full of abominations and filthiness of her fornication: and upon her forehead was a name written, MYSTERY, BABYLON THE GREAT, THE MOTHER Of HARLOTS AND ABOMINATIONS Of THE EARTH. (Revelation 17:1–5)

Exodus chapter 12 continues:

And the blood shall be to you for a token upon the houses where ye are: and when I see the blood, I will pass over you, and the plague shall not be upon you to destroy you, when I smite the land of Egypt. And this day shall be unto you for a memorial; and ye shall keep it a feast to the LORD throughout your generations; ye shall keep it a feast by an ordinance for ever. Seven days shall ye eat unleavened bread; even the first day ye shall put away leaven out of your houses: for whosoever eateth leavened bread from the first day until the seventh day, that soul shall be cut off from Israel. And in the first day there shall be an holy convocation, and in the seventh day there shall be an holy convocation to you; no manner of work shall be done in them, save that which every man must eat, that only may be done of you.

And ye shall observe the feast of unleavened bread; for in this selfsame day have I brought your armies out of the land of Egypt: therefore, shall ye observe this day in your generations by an ordinance for ever. In the first month, on the fourteenth day of the month at even, ye shall eat unleavened bread, until the one and twentieth day of the month at even. Seven days shall there be no leaven found in your houses: for whosoever eateth that which is leavened, even that soul shall be cut off from the congregation of Israel, whether he be a stranger, or born in the land. Ye shall eat nothing leavened; in all your habitations shall ye eat unleavened bread.

Then Moses called for all the elders of Israel, and said unto them, "Draw out and take you a lamb according to your families, and kill the Passover. And ye shall take a bunch of hyssop, and dip it in the blood that is in the bason, and strike the lintel and the two side posts with the blood that is in the bason; and none of you shall go out at the door of his house until the morning. For the LORD will pass through to smite the Egyptians; and when he seeth the blood upon the lintel, and on the two side posts, the LORD will pass over the door, and will not suffer the destroyer to come in unto your houses to smite you."

And ye shall observe this thing for an ordinance to thee and to thy sons for ever. And it shall come to pass, when ye be come to the land which the LORD will give you, according as he hath promised, that ye shall keep this service. And it shall come to pass, when your children shall say unto you, "What mean ye by this service?" That ye shall say, "It is the sacrifice of the LORD's Passover, who passed over the houses of the children of Israel in Egypt, when he smote the Egyptians, and delivered our houses." And the people bowed the head and worshipped. And the children of Israel went away, and did as the LORD had commanded Moses and Aaron, so did they.

And it came to pass, that at midnight the LORD smote all the firstborn in the land of Egypt, from the firstborn of Pharaoh that sat on his throne unto the firstborn of the captive that was in the dungeon; and all the firstborn of cattle. And Pharaoh rose up in the night, he, and all his servants, and all the Egyptians; and there was a great cry in Egypt; for there was not a house where there was not one dead. And he called for Moses and Aaron by night, and said, "Rise up, and get you forth from among my people, both ye and the children of Israel; and go, serve the LORD, as ye have said. Also take your flocks and your herds, as ye have said, and be gone; and bless me also."

And the Egyptians were urgent upon the people, that they might send them out of the land in haste; for they said, "We be all dead men." And the people took their dough before it was leavened, their kneading troughs being bound up in their clothes upon their shoulders. And the children of Israel did according to the word of Moses; and they borrowed of the Egyptians jewels of silver, and jewels of gold, and raiment: and the LORD gave the people favour in the sight of the Egyptians, so that they lent unto them such things as they required. And they spoiled the Egyptians.

And the children of Israel journeyed from Rameses to Succoth, about six hundred thousand on foot that were men, beside children. And a mixed multitude went up also with them; and flocks, and herds, even very much cattle. And they baked unleavened cakes of the dough which they brought forth out of Egypt, for it was not leavened; because they were thrust out of Egypt, and could not tarry, neither had they prepared for themselves any victual.

Now the sojourning of the children of Israel, who dwelt in Egypt, was four hundred and thirty years. And it came to pass at the end of the four hundred and thirty years, even the selfsame day it came to pass, that all the hosts of the LORD went out from the land of Egypt. It is a night to be much observed unto the LORD for bringing them out from the land of Egypt: this is that night of the LORD to be observed of all the children of Israel in their generations.

And the LORD said unto Moses and Aaron, "This is the ordinance of the Passover:"

"There shall no stranger eat thereof: but every man's servant that is bought for money, when thou hast circumcised him, then shall he eat thereof. A foreigner and a hired servant shall not eat thereof."

"In one house shall it be eaten; thou shalt not carry forth ought of the flesh abroad out of the house; neither shall ye break a bone thereof. All the congregation of Israel shall keep it."

"And when a stranger shall sojourn with thee, and will keep the Passover to the LORD, let all his males be circumcised, and then let him come near and keep it; and he shall be as one that is born in the land: for no uncircumcised person shall eat thereof. One law shall be to him that is homeborn, and unto the stranger that sojourneth among you."

Thus did all the children of Israel; as the LORD commanded Moses and Aaron, so did they. And it came to pass the selfsame day, that the LORD did bring the children of Israel out of the land of Egypt by their armies. (Exodus 12:13–51)

So once Israel was freed from four hundred years of slavery, this is how they understood that deliverance— by being disobedient to God and Moses and making a "golden calf" to worship. Because of this, God would destroy many of them.

God made righteous laws and ordinances for His people Israel to be governed by called the Ten Commandments. The Ten Commandments was the most righteous law that He gave the Jews for that period of time. (You might ask yourself why God gave them only ten commandments. Maybe because they couldn't do eleven?)

There is therefore now no condemnation to them which are in Christ Jesus, who walk not after the flesh, but after the Spirit. For the law of the Spirit of life in Christ Jesus hath made me free from the law of sin and death. For what the law could not do, in that it was weak through the flesh, God sending his own Son in the likeness of sinful flesh, and for sin, condemned sin in the flesh: that the righteousness of the law might be fulfilled in us, who walk not after the flesh, but after the Spirit. (Romans 8:1–4)

The Jews had caveman-like minds, or minds like those of two-year-olds. I can relate to raising children at the tender age of two and it goes something like this: I told you not to do that, or to stay out of those cabinets, get out of that toilet, don't eat that dirt—no, no, no, no, please stop. Did you hurt yourself? Ah, but I told you not to.

Now, after all of that they still go into the wrong direction of life? I can feel for the Lord when reading the Bible how He had to raise His family of Israel.

And God spake all these words, saying,

I am the LORD thy God, which have brought thee out of the land of Egypt, out of the house of bondage.

Thou shalt have no other gods before me.

Thou shalt not make unto thee any graven image, or any likeness of anything that is in heaven above, or that is in the earth beneath, or that is in the water under the earth: Thou shalt not bow down thyself to them, nor serve them: for I the LORD thy God am a jealous God, visiting the iniquity of the fathers upon the children unto the third and fourth generation of them that hate me; and shewing mercy unto thousands of them that love me, and keep my commandments.

Thou shalt not take the name of the LORD thy God in vain; for the LORD will not hold him guiltless that taketh his name in vain.

Remember the sabbath day, to keep it holy. Six days shalt thou labour, and do all thy work: but the seventh day is the sabbath of the LORD thy God: in it thou shalt not do any work, thou, nor thy son, nor thy daughter, thy manservant, nor thy maidservant, nor thy cattle, nor thy stranger that is within thy gates: for in six days the LORD made heaven and earth, the sea, and all that in them is, and rested the seventh day: wherefore the LORD blessed the sabbath day, and hallowed it.

Honour thy father and thy mother: that thy days may be long upon the land which the LORD thy God giveth thee.

Thou shalt not kill.

Thou shalt not commit adultery.

Thou shalt not steal.

Thou shalt not bear false witness against thy neighbour.

Thou shalt not covet thy neighbour's house, thou shalt not covet thy neighbour's wife, nor his manservant, nor his maidservant, nor his ox, nor his ass, nor any thing that is thy neighbour's.

And all the people saw the thunderings, and the lightnings, and the noise of the trumpet, and the mountain smoking: and when the people saw it, they removed, and stood afar off. And they said unto Moses, "Speak thou with us, and we will hear: but let not God speak with us, lest we die." And Moses said unto the people, "Fear not: for God is come to prove you, and that his fear may be before your faces, that ye sin not." (Exodus 20:1–20)

Israel Makes a "Golden Calf"

And when the people saw that Moses delayed to come down out of the mount, the people gathered themselves together unto Aaron, and said unto him, "Up, make us gods, which shall go before us; for as for this Moses, the man that brought us up out of the land of Egypt, we wot not what is become of him."

And Aaron said unto them, "Break off the golden earrings, which are in the ears of your wives, of your sons, and of your daughters, and bring them unto me." And all the people brake off the golden earrings which were in their ears, and brought them unto Aaron. And he received them at their hand, and fashioned it with a graving tool, after he had made it a molten calf: and they said, "These be thy gods, O Israel, which brought thee up out of the land of Egypt."

And when Aaron saw it, he built an altar before it; and Aaron made proclamation, and said, "Tomorrow is a feast to the LORD." And they rose up early on the morrow, and offered burnt offerings, and brought peace offerings; and the people sat down to eat and to drink, and rose up to play.

And the LORD said unto Moses, "Go, get thee down; for thy people, which thou broughtest out of the land of Egypt, have corrupted themselves: they have turned aside quickly out of the way which I commanded them: they have made them a molten calf, and have worshipped it, and have sacrificed thereunto, and said, These be thy gods, O Israel, which have brought thee up out of the land of Egypt."

And the LORD said unto Moses, "I have seen this people, and, behold, it is a stiff-necked people: now therefore let me alone, that my wrath may wax hot against them, and that I may consume them: and I will make of thee a great nation." (Exodus 32:1–10)

God's Judgment for Idolatry

"And it came to pass, as soon as he came nigh unto the camp, that he saw the calf, and the dancing: and Moses' anger waxed hot, and he cast the tables out of his hands, and brake them beneath the mount. And he took the calf which they had made, and burnt it in the fire, and ground it to powder, and strawed it upon the water, and made the children of Israel drink of it" (Exodus 32:19–20).

And when Moses saw that the people were naked; (for Aaron had made them naked unto their shame among their enemies:) then Moses stood in the gate of the camp, and said, "Who is on the LORD's side?

let him come unto me." And all the sons of Levi gathered themselves together unto him.

And he said unto them, "Thus saith the LORD God of Israel, Put every man his sword by his side, and go in and out from gate to gate throughout the camp, and slay every man his brother, and every man his companion, and every man his neighbour." And the children of Levi did according to the word of Moses: and there fell of the people that day about three thousand men. (Exodus 32:25–28)

Understand therefore, that the LORD thy God giveth thee not this good land to possess it for thy righteousness; for thou art a stiff-necked people. (Deuteronomy 9:6)

The character traits of the Jews were far different than their "forefathers" Abraham, Isaac, and Jacob in that they were not stubborn or rebellious in nature but obedient men of faith in God. This type of lifestyle literally plagued the Jewish nation even to the coming of Christ. They continually disobeyed the commandments of God by whoredoms with other countries and sacrificing to idols. This was wrong because the other countries would have the Jews worshipping their idols, and this was called spiritual fornication.

God Divorces Israel due to Idolatry

And the LORD said unto me, "The backsliding Israel hath justified herself more than treacherous Judah. Go and proclaim these words toward the north, and say, Return, thou backsliding Israel," saith the LORD; "and I will not cause mine anger to fall upon you: for I am merciful, saith the LORD, and I will not keep anger for ever. Only acknowledge thine iniquity, that thou hast transgressed against the LORD thy God, and hast scattered thy ways to the strangers under every green tree, and ye have not obeyed my voice," saith the LORD. [No matter how hard the Lord punished Israel, they weren't going to

116

change or repent, so God would allow a country to capture them and put the Jews in bondage to the fourth beast, Rome.] "Turn, O backsliding children, saith the LORD; for I am married unto you: and I will take you one of a city, and two of a family, and I will bring you to Zion: and I will give you pastors according to mine heart, which shall feed you with knowledge and understanding. And it shall come to pass, when ye be multiplied and increased in the land, in those days," saith the LORD, "They shall say no more, The ark of the covenant of the LORD: neither shall it come to mind: neither shall they remember it; neither shall they visit it; neither shall that be done any more." (Jeremiah 3:11–16)

God Seeks Another "Wife" – The Gentiles – and a New Law

Behold, the days come, saith the LORD, that I will make a new covenant with the house of Israel, and with the house of Judah: not according to the covenant that I made with their fathers in the day that I took them by the hand to bring them out of the land of Egypt; which my covenant they brake, although I was an husband unto them, saith the LORD: But this shall be the covenant that I will make with the house of Israel; After those days, saith the LORD, I will put my law in their inward parts, and write it in their hearts; and will be their God, and they shall be my people. And they shall teach no more every man his neighbour, and every man his brother, saying, "Know the LORD: for they shall all know me, from the least of them unto the greatest of them, saith the LORD: for I will forgive their iniquity, and I will remember their sin no more." (Jeremiah 31:31–34)

The New Testament for a New People of God,

No More Israel "And I say unto you, Whosoever shall put away his wife, except it be for fornication, and shall marry another, committeth adultery: and whoso marrieth her which is put away doth commit adultery" (Matthew 19:9). God had the physical and spiritual right to "divorce" Israel for committing physical and spiritual adultery with other countries' idols and women.

For Zion's sake will I not hold my peace, and for Jerusalem's sake I will not rest, until the righteousness thereof go forth as brightness, and the salvation thereof as a lamp that burneth. And the Gentiles shall see thy righteousness, and all kings thy glory: and thou shalt be called by a new name, which the mouth of the LORD shall name. (Isaiah 62:1–2)

No Man Has Seen God

This almighty God, Jehovah or Yahweh, is invisible, so you can't make images of Him.

And the LORD said "Unto Moses, I will do this thing also that thou hast spoken: for thou hast found grace in my sight, and I know thee by name."

And he said, "I beseech thee, shew me thy glory."

And he said, "I will make all my goodness pass before thee, and I will proclaim the name of the LORD before thee; and will be gracious to whom I will be gracious, and will shew mercy on whom I will shew mercy." And he said, "Thou canst not see my face: for there shall no man see me, and live."

And the LORD said, "Behold, there is a place by me, and thou shalt stand upon a rock: and it shall come to pass, while my glory passeth by, that I will put thee in a clift of the rock, and will cover thee with my hand while I pass by: and I will take away mine hand, and thou shalt see my back parts: but my face shall not be seen." (Exodus 33:17–23)

"No man hath seen God at any time; the only begotten Son, which is in the bosom of the father, he hath declared him" (John 1:18). You can't worship this God with any form of idolatry such as Rosary beads, crosses made of wood, silver, or gold, or any medallions. What about looking up to heaven and making a symbol of a cross with your hands across your chest or rubbing your medallion on your necklace or the like?

21(for all the Athenians and strangers which were there spent their time in nothing else, but either to tell, or to hear some new thing.)

Then Paul stood in the midst of Mars' hill, and said, "Ye men of Athens, I perceive that in all things ye are too superstitious. For as I passed by, and beheld your devotions, I found an altar with this inscription, TO THE UNKNOWN GOD. Whom therefore ye ignorantly worship, him declare I unto you."

God that made the world and all things therein, seeing that he is Lord of heaven and earth, dwelleth not in temples made with hands; neither is worshipped with men's hands, as though he needed anything, seeing he giveth to all life, and breath, and all things; and hath made of one blood all nations of men for to dwell on all the face of the earth, and hath determined the times before appointed, and the bounds of their habitation; that they should seek the Lord, if haply they might feel after him, and find him, though he be not far from every one of us. (Acts 17:21-27)

God wants to be worshipped His way or the highway.

God tells you the name of His "wife" and not vice versa. Oh, I founded this building so I'm going to name this church after me or let me just pick out a name in the bible or draw straws," etc. Remember, God always named His people. Do you remember reading (because "faith comes by hearing and hearing by the word of God") where God changed the name of Abram to Abraham, Sarai to Sarah, Jacob to Israel, and Saul to Paul the apostle? Don't you get it that if names are not written in the Bible, you shouldn't have faith in them?

So, when you read the Bible, where do you find these names to believe in or to have faith in? Catholic, Baptist, Jehovah's Witnesses, Methodist, AME Zion, the Holiness religions, Mormons, illuminati, Buddha, Confucius, Christian Scientist, Scientology, Muslims, Seventh-Day Adventist, Episcopal, Presbyterian, Nondenominations, All faiths, and the like?

The "Wife of Christ"

Most people don't know that Jesus Christ is married, but to whom?

So, let's take a simple look at marriage comparisons. As God was a "husband" to the Jews, so is Christ to his "wife," the church. This is very simple. When a man marries a woman, the woman takes on the man's name in natural culture today. "Unto the woman he said, I will greatly multiply thy sorrow and thy conception; in sorrow thou shalt bring forth children; and thy desire shall be to thy husband, and he shall rule over thee" (Genesis 3:16).

Wives, submit yourselves unto your own husbands, as unto the Lord.

For the husband is the head of the wife, even as Christ is the head of the church: and the savior of the body. Therefore, as the church is subject unto Christ, so let the wives be to their own husbands in everything. Husbands, love your wives, even as Christ also loved the church, and gave himself for it;

That he might sanctify and cleanse it with the washing of the water by the word,

That he might present it to himself a glorious church, not having spot, or wrinkle, or any such thing, but that it should be holy and without blemish.,

So, ought men to love their wives as their own flesh, but nourisheth and cherisheth it, even as the Lord the church:

For we are members of his body, of his flesh, and of his bones.

For this cause shall a man leave his father and mother, and shall be joined unto his wife, and they two shall be one flesh.

This is a great mystery but I speak concerning Christ and the church. (Ephesians 5:22–32) So, having said that, Jesus Christ's last name isn't any of those just listed. above.

Jesus Himself said, "For many shall come in my name, saying, I am Christ; and shall deceive many." (Matthew 24:5).

"One" – Compare Old Testament and New Testament

Remember now how "orderly" God is in everything that He does. In the Old Testament there was: •

One God that was invisible

- One wife named Israel

- One faith in this invisible God in heaven

- One Law – the Ten Commandments

How to Become a Jew

One becomes a Jew by birth through the lineage of "Abraham's seed," which was Isaac and Jacob. Then Jacob had twelve sons, and Jacob's name was changed to Israel, and his sons became the patriarchs of the twelve tribes of Israel.

Proselyte Jews

Proselyte Jews are not Jews by birth but come from another people and denounce their religion of idolatry to serve the Jewish invisible God Jehovah. This is basically called "Jewish citizenship," and you do all the things according to the Jewish religion.

Woe unto you, scribes and Pharisees, hypocrites! for ye compass sea and land to make one proselyte, and when he is made, ye make him twofold more the child of hell than yourselves. (Matthew 23:15)

And the saying pleased the whole multitude: and they chose Stephen, a man full of faith and of the Holy Ghost, and Philip, and Prochorus, and Nicanor, and Timon, and Parmenas, and Nicolas a proselyte of Antioch. (Acts 6:5)

What Must a Jew Do to Be Saved under the Old Testament?

Circumcision

Circumcision is when the foreskin of the male's penis is cut away for cleanliness, due to possible germs and infections to the female and new born. God was a doctor to man because He created him, and God knew all of the ins and outs of man. No other countries knew about circumcision but the Jews, because they were God's chosen people at that time.

So, the other countries were called uncircumcised or unclean, and they were also called Gentiles. What would happen to the other countries due to not being circumcised is that the female would get an infection and pass it on to the fetus, which may become deformed. Diseases were rampant in these other countries, being passed down through their children.

The "Seed" of Abraham

Now, who was to come through the "seed" of Abraham? The Lord and Savior of the world was coming through the seed of Abraham, so His lineage needed to be pure and clean to prepare for the birth of the Christ.

Abraham and His Family Circumcised

And when Abram was ninety years old and nine, the LORD appeared to Abram, and said unto him, "I am the Almighty God; walk before me, and be thou perfect."

2 "And I will make my covenant between me and thee, and will multiply thee exceedingly."

And Abram fell on his face: and God talked with him, saying,

4 "As for me, behold, my covenant is with thee, and thou shalt be a father of many nations."

5 "Neither shall thy name any more be called Abram, but thy name shall be Abraham; for a father of many nations have I made thee."

6 "And I will make thee exceeding fruitful, and I will make nations of thee, and kings shall come out of thee."

7 "And I will establish my covenant between me and thee and thy seed after thee in their generations for an everlasting covenant, to be a God unto thee, and to thy seed after thee."

8 "And I will give unto thee, and to thy seed after thee, the land wherein thou art a stranger, all the land of Canaan, for an everlasting possession; and I will be their God."

9And God said unto Abraham, "Thou shalt keep my covenant therefore, thou, and thy seed after thee in their generations. This is my covenant, which ye shall keep, between me and you and thy seed after thee; Every man child among you shall be circumcised. And ye shall circumcise the flesh of your foreskin; and it shall be a token of the covenant betwixt me and you. And he that is eight days old shall be circumcised among you, every man child in your generations, he that is born in the house, or bought with money of any stranger, which is not of thy seed. He that is born in thy house, and he that is bought with thy money, must needs be circumcised: and my covenant shall be in your flesh for an everlasting covenant. And the uncircumcised man child whose flesh of his foreskin is not circumcised, that soul shall be cut off from his people; he hath broken my covenant."

And God said unto Abraham, "As for Sarai thy wife, thou shalt not call her name Sarai, but Sarah shall her name be. And I will bless her, and give thee a son also of her: yea, I will bless her, and she shall be a mother of nations; kings of people shall be of her."

Then Abraham fell upon his face, and laughed, and said in his heart, "Shall a child be born unto him that is an hundred years old? And shall Sarah, that is ninety years old, bear?" And Abraham said unto God, "O that Ishmael might live before thee!"

And God said, "Sarah thy wife shall bear thee a son indeed; and thou shalt call his name Isaac: and I will establish my covenant with him for an everlasting covenant, and with his seed after him. And as for Ishmael, I have heard thee: Behold, I have blessed him, and will make him fruitful, and will multiply him exceedingly; twelve princes shall he beget, and I will make him a great nation. But my covenant will I establish with Isaac, which Sarah shall bear unto thee at this set time in the next year." And he left off talking with him, and God went up from Abraham.

And Abraham took Ishmael his son, and all that were born in his house, and all that were bought with his money, every male among the men of Abraham's house; and circumcised the flesh of their foreskin in the selfsame day, as God had said unto him. And Abraham was ninety years old and nine, when he was circumcised in the flesh of his foreskin. And Ishmael his son was thirteen years old, when he was circumcised in the flesh of his foreskin. In the selfsame day was Abraham circumcised, and Ishmael his son. And all the men of his house, born in the house, and bought with money of the stranger, were circumcised with him. (Genesis 17:1–27)

No Politics

In the Jewish community there was no politics or people running for an office. God ordained Moses as the Lawgiver/Judge and elders from every tribe and a priesthood called the Levitical priesthood, and in time there would be judges leading the people.

"Spiritual Circumcision" under the New Testament in the New Testament there is unity.

There is one body, and one Spirit, even as ye are called in one hope of your calling; one Lord, one faith, one baptism, one God and father of all, who is above all, and through all, and in you all. (Ephesians 4:4–6)

Submitting yourselves one to another in the fear of God.

Wives, submit yourselves unto your own husbands, as unto the Lord. [No other man can tell your wife what to do; even if your wife becomes president, queen, or CEO, she is subject to her husband in all things.] For the husband is the head of the wife, even as Christ is the head of the church: and he is the saviour of the body. [The husband is the savior of his wife and children.] Therefore, as the church is subject unto Christ, so let the wives be to their own husbands in every thing.

Husbands, love your wives, even as Christ also loved the church, and gave himself for it; that he might sanctify and cleanse it with the washing of water by the word, that he might present it to himself a glorious church, not having spot, or wrinkle, or any such thing; but that it should be holy and without blemish [a clean, spiritual wife]. So, ought men to love their wives as their own bodies. He that loveth his wife loveth himself. For no man ever yet hated his own flesh; but nourisheth and cherisheth it, even as the Lord the church: for we are members of his body, of his flesh, and of his bones. For this cause shall a man leave his father and mother, and shall be joined unto his wife, and they two shall be one flesh. This is a great mystery: but I speak concerning Christ and the church. [The disciples are married to Jesus; they are his wife, which is the church.] Nevertheless, let every one of you in particular so love his wife even as himself; and the wife see that she reverences her husband. (Ephesians 5:21–33)

Ten Virgins

"Then shall the kingdom of heaven be likened unto ten virgins, which took their lamps, and went forth to meet the bridegroom" (Matthew 25:1). These ten virgins were going to meet Christ to be married, but what I like to take from this is that Jesus wasn't going to marry a woman that had been with another man.

So, Jesus tells you how to be free from sin, and it's not any type of "sinner's prayer." You must also get rid of your last "husband": Catholic, Baptist, Jehovah's Witness, Jewish, Methodist, Seventh-Day Adventist, Muslim, Christian Scientist, Scientology, Buddhist, Confucian, Lutheran, Presbyterian, Episcopal, All faiths, Nondenominations, the Holiness Religions, and the like. You must also get rid of all forms of idolatry and covetousness. The spiritual setting is that the wife of Christ is going to be pure, holy, and without blemish, meaning without sins.

Jesus Christ Builds His Church

When Jesus came into the coasts of Caesarea Philippi, he asked his disciples, saying, "Whom do men say that I the Son of man am?"

And they said, "Some say that thou art John the Baptist: some, Elias; and others, Jeremias, or one of the prophets."

He saith unto them, "But whom say ye that I am?"

And Simon Peter answered and said, "Thou art the Christ, the Son of the living God."

And Jesus answered and said unto him, "Blessed art thou, Simon Barjona: for flesh and blood hath not revealed it unto thee, but my father which is in heaven. And I say also unto thee, that thou art Peter, and upon this rock I will build my church; and the gates of hell shall not prevail against it. [A rock symbolized truth, strong and tough to break, so "Upon that truth I will build my Church or my wife." The wife carries Jesus's name by spiritual marriage.] And I will give unto thee the keys of the kingdom of heaven: and whatsoever thou shalt bind on earth shall be bound in heaven: and whatsoever thou shalt loose on earth shall be loosed in heaven." (Matthew 16:13–19)

The key to this scripture is I (the Son of God), meaning mine (that is, His) and not yours because you don't have the authority to have a church, a spiritual wife, period, and you didn't die on the cross for the sins of the world.

The Lord said, "I will build my church and the gates of hell shall not prevail against it." The gates of hell shall prevail against: Catholic, Baptist, Jehovah's Witness, Jewish, Methodist, and all the rest.

Jesus Is Married

In Revelation 22:17 we read, "And the Spirit and the bride say, Come. And let him that heareth say, Come And let him that is athirst come. And whosoever will, let him take the water of life freely."

Let's say I come to Jesus Christ's house and knock on the door and say, "Does Mrs. Catholic live here?" Or how about "Does Mrs. Baptist live here?" It can't get any simpler than that. The world doesn't get this simple understanding because the world is deceived.

"And a highway shall be there, and a way, and it shall be called the Way of Holiness. The unclean shall not pass over it, but it shall be for those; the wayfaring men, though fools, shall not err therein". (Isaiah 35:8).

The Churches of Christ

"The churches of Christ salute you" (Romans 16:16). Basically, what Paul the apostle is saying is that the churches teaching Jesus's doctrine belong to Christ, and they carry His name.

The Seven Churches

"The mystery of the seven stars which thou sawest in my right hand, and the seven golden candlesticks. The seven stars are the angels of the seven churches: and the seven candlesticks which thou sawest are the seven churches" (Revelation 1:20). Notice how these seven churches are named:

Unto the angel of the church of Ephesus write; These things saith he that holdeth the seven stars in his right hand, who walketh in the midst of the seven golden candlesticks; …

And unto the angel of the church in Smyrna write; These things saith the first and the last, which was dead, and is alive; …

And to the angel of the church in Pergamos write; These things saith he which hath the sharp sword with two edges; …

And unto the angel of the church in Thyatira write; These things saith the Son of God, who hath his eyes like unto a flame of fire, and his feet are like fine brass. (Revelation 2:1, 8, 12, 18)

Jesus Will Punish His Wife

Notwithstanding I have a few things against thee, because thou sufferest that woman Jezebel, which calleth herself a prophetess, to teach and to seduce my servants to commit fornication, and to eat things sacrificed unto idols. And I gave her space to repent of her fornication; and she repented not. Behold, I will cast her into a bed, and them that commit adultery with her into great tribulation, except they repent of their deeds. And I will kill her children with death; and all the churches shall know that I am he which searcheth the reins and hearts: and I will give unto every one of you according to your works.

But unto you I say, and unto the rest in Thyatira, as many as have not this doctrine, and which have not known the depths of Satan, as they speak; I will put upon you none other burden. (Revelation 2:20–24)

And unto the angel of the church in Sardis write; These things saith he that hath the seven Spirits of God, and the seven stars; I know thy works, that thou hast a name that thou livest, and art dead ....

And to the angel of the church in Philadelphia write; These things saith he that is holy, he that is true, he that hath the key of David, he that openeth, and no man shutteth; and shutteth, and no man openeth; …

And unto the angel of the church of the Laodiceans write; These things saith the Amen, the faithful and true witness, the beginning of the creation of God. (Revelation 3:1, 7, 14)

The Lord Rebukes His Wife in Love

As many as I love, I rebuke and chasten: be zealous therefore, and repent. Behold, I stand at the door, and knock: if any man hear my voice, and open the door, I will come in to him, and will sup with him, and he with me.

To him that overcometh will I grant to sit with me in my throne, even as I also overcame, and am set down with my father in his throne. He that hath an ear, let him hear what the Spirit saith unto the churches. (Revelation 3:19–22)

Revelation 3 assures us that Jesus's rebuke is in love.

ONE WIFE

Although there were seven (7) churches in different cities they represent one wife, which is the church, meaning "one body." "For as the body is one, and hath many members, and all the members of that one body, being many, are one body: so also, is Christ" (1 Corinthians 12:12). Meaning: The Lord being the head, the apostles, elders, deacons, teachers, prophets, and disciples make up the church. "There is one body, and one Spirit, even as ye are called in one hope of your calling" (Ephesians 4:4).

Adding to the Name of Christ Is a "Curse"

As you have read, there is no such animal as the Catholic Church or Baptist Church and the like because you have added a name before the Lord's wife's name.

Ye shall not add unto the word which I command you, neither shall ye diminish ought from it, that ye may keep the commandments of the LORD your God which I command you. (Deuteronomy 4:2)

For I testify unto every man that heareth the words of the prophecy of this book, if any man shall add unto these things, God shall add unto him the plagues that are written in this book: and if any man shall take away from the words of the book of this prophecy, God shall take away his part out of the book of life, and out of the holy city, and from the things which are written in this book. (Revelation 22:18–19)

Jesus Christ started the first church in history, and everyone else is a copycat, meaning a false-teaching church; therefore, against these other so-called churches the gates of hell will prevail. Jesus is telling you what's going to happen to these other religions that will spring up in time.

False-Teaching Churches

This scripture of prophecy really opened my eyes to understanding as to when Jesus started his church, so see if you understand this scripture.

The word that Isaiah the son of Amoz saw concerning Judah and Jerusalem. And it shall come to pass in the last days, that the mountain of the LORD's house shall be established in the top of the mountains, and shall be exalted above the hills; and all nations shall flow unto it. And many people shall go and say, "Come ye, and let us go up to the mountain of the LORD, to the house of the God of Jacob; and he will teach us of his ways, and we will walk in his paths: for out of Zion shall go forth the law, and the word of the LORD from Jerusalem." (Isaiah 2:1–3)

Jesus said, "Go ye into all the world, and preach the gospel to every creature. He that believeth and is baptized shall be saved; but he that believeth not shall be damned" (Mark 16:15–16). Now Jesus, being the head of His church and the first one to start a church, fulfills this scripture because Jesus said while in Jerusalem, "Go into all the world and preach my gospel (law) to every creature," did He not?

131

My next point then is when did these "copycat religions" start and where? Why? Because these other religions didn't start in Jerusalem, and they didn't start the "New Testament" from Jerusalem, as did Jesus Christ. The teachings of the New Testament started in Jerusalem, and the first church started in Jerusalem, so if your church that you belong to now didn't start in Jerusalem and didn't make any laws from Jerusalem, then you belong to a false-teaching church.

Everything Started in Jerusalem

You must be very careful when reading commentaries as well as online searches because they can lead you astray. This is cleverly done by Satan to deceive you. The Roman Catholic Church started some hundreds of years after the death of Jesus Christ, and they are from Rome, which is the fourth beast, and they crucified the Lord. So Rome's laws were like night to day when talking about righteousness, because it was Rome who crucified a sinless man and let a robber go free and is now taking his place by deceit, "who opposeth and exalteth himself above all that is called God, or that is worshipped; so that he as God sitteth in the temple of God, shewing himself that he is God" (2 Thessalonians 2:4). This is the pope, who is the "son of perdition."

The first Baptist Church was started by a man named Roger Williams in America in the year 1603. This is some 1600 years after Jesus started His church from Jerusalem. The Methodist Church was started by John Wesley in the eighteenth century in England, some 1700 years after Jesus started His church. The Lutheran Church was started by Martin Luther in the sixteenth century in Germany, not in Jerusalem some two thousand years ago. These and many other religious doctrines didn't start from Jerusalem some two thousand years ago because the prophecy started there, according to Isaiah.

In Mark 16:15, Jesus said, "Go into all the world and preach the gospel to every creature, meaning Rome, Africa, Egypt, Asia, Greece,

Britain, Germany, and the like need to be saved. White, black, red, yellow, and green people need to be saved because "all have sinned": "for all have sinned, and come short of the glory of God" (Romans 3:23). Everyone has sinned. The color of your skin doesn't make you better than any other color.

Black Congregations?

The European white congregations such as Catholics, Baptist, Methodist, and the like didn't want any African slaves to be members of their religions. So, the slaves basically took on the religions of their masters. If the slave master was a Baptist, then the slave would become a Baptist.

Now since the slaves couldn't worship with the white congregations, they made their own "black Baptist" congregations, thereby copying the white congregations' "religions." for example the Methodist "churches" didn't want blacks in their religious gatherings, so the blacks started the "AME Zion" religion. The AME Zion or African Methodist Episcopal Zion Organization was started in 1821 in New York City.

Copying for Salvation?

I was an A-B Honor Roll student from the first grade to the twelfth grade, but I didn't get there by being dumb. I had a "political" side to me—copying, if you want to call it that. Let's say John Doe was an A-B student too, and I would say, "Hey, Doe, now the two main political parties in the United States are 'Democrats and the Republicans', right? So, the 'independent Party' wouldn't be one of these in the answer to question number 9, right?"

In getting to heaven you don't want to copy dummies, such as people who stole your land and took it by force, burned crosses in your yard, burned down your houses, killed and raped you, gave you a higher interest rate because you were black, wouldn't give you credit or lynched you five and ten at a time like you were at a barbecue, all in the name of Jesus Christ.

My mom told the story when she was a young girl working for some whites in Alabama, the man tried to rape her, so she had to break out of the house to be saved. My question to the black congregations is why in this "hell" do you think that the white people are the only ones that know how to be saved? What possessed you as a black to think that? "Yes'm, boss." You still would have been wrong if you'd said, "We'll call our congregation the Church of Ethiopia or Nigeria or Mozambique," but instead you copied the wrong student. Read Romans 10:17: "So then faith cometh by hearing, and hearing by the word of God." Where are these faiths mentioned above in the Bible? And John 17:17: "Sanctify them through thy truth: thy word is truth." Set the apostle apart from the world by thy word which is truth. Nowhere did the Apostle teach these beliefs.

Jesus said, "For many shall come in my name, saying, I am Christ; and shall deceive many" (Matthew 24:5).

An African Was Saved Two Thousand Years Ago

The Ethiopian eunuch was saved. The Lord wanted this man to be saved:

And the angel of the Lord spake unto Philip, saying, "Arise, and go toward the south unto the way that goeth down from Jerusalem unto Gaza, which is desert." And he arose and went: and, behold, a man of Ethiopia, an eunuch of great authority under Candace queen of the Ethiopians, who had the charge of all her treasure, and had come to Jerusalem for to worship, was returning, and sitting in his chariot read Esaias the prophet. [Remember that we discussed Proselyte Jews; this

Ethiopian eunuch was one.] Then the Spirit said unto Philip, "Go near, and join thyself to this chariot." [Philip didn't say, "Not so, my Lord, because this man is a black man."]

And Philip ran thither to him, and heard him read the prophet Esaias, and said, "Understandest thou what thou readest?"

And he said, H"ow can I, except some man should guide me?" And he desired Philip that he would come up and sit with him.

The place of the scripture which he read was this, He was led as a sheep to the slaughter; and like a lamb dumb before his shearer, so opened he not his mouth: in his humiliation his judgment was taken away: and who shall declare his generation? for his life is taken from the earth.

And the eunuch answered Philip, and said, "I pray thee, of whom speaketh the prophet this? of himself, or of some other man?" Then Philip opened his mouth, and began at the same scripture, and preached unto him Jesus.

And as they went on their way, they came unto a certain water: and the eunuch said, "See, here is water; what doth hinder me to be baptized?" And Philip said, "If thou believest with all thine heart, thou mayest." And he answered and said, "I believe that Jesus Christ is the Son of God." And he commanded the chariot to stand still: and they went down both into the water, both Philip and the eunuch; and he baptized him. And when they were come up out of the water, the Spirit of the Lord caught away Philip, that the eunuch saw him no more: and he went on his way rejoicing. (Acts 8:26–39)

The almighty God wanted everyone to be saved, and He didn't do this by accident to put the example of the Ethiopian eunuch in the Bible. God knows everything, including the future and how Africans would be treated in this life.

- "And the name of the second river is Gihon: the same is it that compasseth the whole land of Ethiopia" (Genesis 2:13). Ethiopia is mentioned in the beginning of time. God made the "Ethiopian."

- "Can the Ethiopian change his skin, or the leopard his spots? Then may ye also do good, that are accustomed to do evil" (Jeremiah 13:23).

- "Are ye not as children of the Ethiopians unto me, O children of Israel? saith the LORD. Have not I brought up Israel out of the land of Egypt? and the Philistines from Caphtor, and the Syrians from Kir?" (Amos 9:7).

"You mean some people from Africa will be in heaven? Get out of here."

God Isn't a Racist

"After this I beheld, and, lo, a great multitude, which no man could number, of all nations, and kindreds, and people, and tongues, stood before the throne, and before the Lamb, clothed with white robes, and palms in their hands" (Revelation 7:9).

When you call people by many names like wetback, the N word, slant-eye, redskin, Jap, coon, and the like, you are talking about the Almighty God.

My Hope Is in This

"Dearly beloved, avenge not yourselves, but rather give place unto wrath: for it is written, Vengeance is mine; I will repay, saith the Lord" (Romans 12:19).

We humbly go about our daily lives in this America. "And [God] hath made of one blood all nations of men for to dwell on all the face of the earth, and hath determined the times before appointed, and the bounds of their habitation" (Acts 17:26).

You cannot name a church after the apostles. You may drive around town and see on a church sign "The Apostolic Church." Now when I pray, I don't say "in the name of Paul" or Peter or any of the apostles. Why? Because none of them died on the cross for my sins; none was the savior of the world, so they can't have a church named after them.

John 14:13

"And whatsoever ye shall ask in My name, that will I do, that the Father may be glorified in the Son."

John the Apostle Watches the Crucifixion of Christ

Now there stood by the cross of Jesus his mother, and his mother's sister, Mary the wife of Cleophas, and Mary Magdalene. When Jesus therefore saw his mother, and the disciple standing by, whom he loved, he saith unto his mother, Woman, behold thy son! Then saith he to the disciple, Behold thy mother! (John 19:25–27)

My point here is that most of the apostles had fled for fear of persecution, but you have John watching the crucifixion and being told by Christ to take care of His mother, Mary.

No Other Name on the Marquee but Christ

The apostle Paul tells the Corinthians why they can't use his name for salvation:

For it hath been declared unto me of you, my brethren, by them which are of the house of Chloe, that there are contentions among you. Now this I say, that every one of you saith, I am of Paul; and I of Apollos; and I of Cephas; and I of Christ. is Christ divided? Was Paul crucified for you? or were ye baptized in the name of Paul? I thank God that I baptized none of you, but Crispus and Gaius; lest any should say that I had baptized in mine own name. (1 Corinthians 1:11–15)

What about Saint Peter's Basilica or Saint Paul's Cathedral? The apostle Paul reiterates that you can't put his name on anything that pertains to Jesus Christ: "Neither is there salvation in any other: for there is none other name under heaven given among men, whereby we must be saved" (Acts 4:12). "For this cause I bow my knees unto the father of our Lord Jesus Christ, of whom the whole family in heaven and earth is named" (Ephesians 3:14–15). "And Jesus came and spake unto them, saying, All power is given unto me in heaven and in earth" (Matthew 28:18).

If Jesus is the savior, why then are we building buildings in the name of the apostles? When we pray, we don't ask anything in the name of the apostles; we say in "Jesus's name."

This was done by Rome, the fourth beast, to deceive.

"Wresting the Scriptures"

Twisting:

As also in all his [Paul's] epistles, speaking in them of these things; in which are some things hard to be understood, which they that are unlearned and unstable wrest, as they do also the other scriptures, unto their own destruction. (2 Peter 3:16)

There is great damnation for men who wrest or twist the Word of God. "For the prophecy came not in old time by the will of man: but holy men of God spake as they were moved by the Holy Ghost." (2 Peter 1:21)

Fact from Fiction

You can continue these searches of religions, and you will not find that any of them came from Jerusalem some two thousand years ago because God made sure that His Son started the first church from the prophecies of Isaiah 2:2. So if Jesus is married to His wife, then the wife takes on Jesus's name. "As he saith also in Osee [Hosea], I will call them my people, which were not my people [the Gentiles]; and her beloved, which was not beloved" (Romans 9:25). "And the Gentiles shall see thy righteousness, and all kings thy glory: and thou shalt be called by a new name, which the mouth of the LORD shall name" (Isaiah 62:2). "And ye shall leave your name for a curse unto my chosen: for the Lord GOD shall slay thee, and call his servants by another name" (Isaiah 65:15). No more Israel or Jews: God divorced Israel and married another people.

Religious Names on the Marquee

Jesus Christ is the head of the church, and He died for the world, but His name isn't on the marquees. Do this when you go to worship at your prospective place. Look and see whose name is on the Marquee, the church sign. By that fact, when you see another name on the marquee, this will let you know where you are going.

And Jesus came and spake unto them, saying, "All power is given unto me in heaven and in earth." [Everything is Jesus. Does any type of "light" come on upstairs?] "Go ye therefore, and teach all nations, baptizing them in the name of the father, and of the Son, and of the Holy Ghost: teaching them to observe all things whatsoever I have commanded you: and, lo, I am with you always, even unto the end of the world. Amen." (Matthew 28:18–20)

Who is the image of the invisible God, the firstborn of every creature: for by him were all things created, that are in heaven, and that are in earth, visible and invisible, whether they be thrones, or dominions, or principalities, or powers: all things were created by him, and for him: and he is before all things, and by him all things consist. And he is the head of the body, the church: who is the beginning, the firstborn from the dead; that in all things he might have the preeminence. [Jesus is the first in everything.] for it pleased the father that in him should all fulness dwell; and, having made peace through the blood of his cross, by him to reconcile all things unto himself; by him, I say, whether they be things in earth, or things in heaven. (Colossians 1:15–20)

"For this cause I bow my knees unto the father of our Lord Jesus Christ, of whom the whole family in heaven and earth is named" (Ephesians 3:14–15). No one gets this and the whole wide world is clueless to the fact that everything in heaven and earth is named after Jesus Christ, today. So where do these popes, archbishops, cardinals, reverends, televangelists, rabbis, doctors of theology, and the like come from? They aren't in the Bible, except rabbis.

Now let's see what the Lord said about rabbis. "But be not ye called Rabbi: for one is your Master, even Christ; and all ye are brethren" (Matthew 23:8). He called for humility, humbleness, meekness, and no pride or ego tripping. "My name is Reverend Doctor So-and-So or Pope John Doe.," or any such labels. How about Cardinals or Archbishops or any such labels? This is nothing but a pyramid scheme.

Rome loved titles, like Augustus Caesar or Emperor. So, if the Lord said no, are you going to go against him?

"Christians"

The believers in Christ take on His name, meaning "belonging to Christ." The believers are married to Jesus Christ. The key phrase in Isaiah 62:2 is "called by a new name, which the mouth of the LORD shall name."

"Then departed Barnabas to Tarsus, for to seek Saul: and when he had found him, he brought him unto Antioch. And it came to pass, that a whole year they assembled themselves with the church, and taught much people. And the disciples were called Christians first in Antioch" (Acts 11:25-26). This is the first time that the name Christians is ever used in the Bible, and these are the believers that God has chosen to be His people. The "wife" of Christ or the church of Christ takes on His last name and becomes Christians.

I used to ask people, "What faith are you?" They might say, "I'm a Catholic or Baptist Christian or Methodist Christian," and the like, but there is no such animal in the Bible. If you add or subtract form the Word of God, you will have sinned, and plagues will be upon you—just as we see across the world today. So, you can't put any name or "prefix" or "suffix" next to the holy name of Christian lest you be cursed.

Ye shall not add unto the word which I command you, neither shall ye diminish ought from it, that ye may keep the commandments of the LORD your God which I command you. (Deuteronomy 4:2)

For I testify unto every man that heareth the words of the prophecy of this book, if any man shall add unto these things, God shall add unto him the plagues that are written in this book: and if any man shall take away from the words of the book of this prophecy, God shall take away his part out of the book of life, and out of the holy city, and from the things which are written in this book. (Revelation 22:18–19)

Salvation – "The Church," the Wife of Christ, and the Kingdom "And the kingdom and dominion, and the greatness of the kingdom under the whole heaven, shall be given to the people of the saints of the most High, whose kingdom is an everlasting kingdom, and all dominions shall serve and obey him" (Daniel 7:27).

The Lord gave Peter the "keys to the kingdom" in Matthew 16:19: "And I will give unto thee the keys of the kingdom of heaven: and whatsoever thou shalt bind on earth shall be bound in heaven: and whatsoever thou shalt loose on earth shall be loosed in heaven." Peter was given authority to carry out the laws within the church.

So how do you become a "believer" or "disciple" in the church? In other words, what must you do to be saved? There is so much false teaching about the answer to that question. "As also in all his [Paul's] epistles, speaking in them of these things; in which are some things hard to be understood, which they that are unlearned and unstable wrest, as they do also the other scriptures, unto their own destruction" (2 Peter 3:16). So, when you twist the word of God to your benefit, you sin, so being a false teacher can take you to hell. "And he spake a parable unto them, Can the blind lead the blind? Shall they not both fall into the ditch?" (Luke 6:39)

Pray the Sinner's Prayer and Accepting Christ in your heart as your personal savior?

There is a teaching called the "sinner's prayer," but have you ever studied this teaching that many televangelists teach? There is no such teaching in the Bible called the "sinner's prayer." Or accepting Christ as your personal Savior. The last time I checked, Jesus died for the world to repent and to be saved so He can't be anyone's personal Savior. It sounds good, but it isn't the truth, because the examples in the Bible don't "corroborate" this lie, and here's why. Let's read what the examples teach us from the Bible.

You have to believe in Jesus's laws to be saved, and not the fourth beast's laws, because the fourth beast is there to lie and to trick you out of your salvation. A lot of ministers teach from this scripture to justify the sinner's prayer in ignorance, because God doesn't hear sinners:

Two men went up into the temple to pray; the one a Pharisee, and the other a publican. The Pharisee stood and prayed thus with himself, God, I thank thee, that I am not as other men are, extortioners, unjust, adulterers, or even as this publican. Fast twice in the week, I give tithes of all that I possess.

142

And the publican, standing afar off, would not lift up so much as his eyes unto heaven, but smote upon his breast, saying, "God be merciful to me a sinner."

I tell you, this man went down to his house justified rather than the other: for everyone that exalteth himself shall be abased; and he that humbleth himself shall be exalted. (Luke 18:10–14)

"Justified" doesn't mean "heard." When you come to God, you must be "simple and true" and not a boaster with pride. Both of these men have sinned because you have a Pharisee, who belonged to a sect with a different belief than what the Jews were taught, and the publican was a tax collector for the Roman Empire, which is the fourth beast. Jesus is teaching his disciples not to be a hypocrite or to cast down someone else because you think you are better than the other person. Jesus doesn't even say that God heard their prayers.

Last is that the Jews always had God's ear when they obeyed, and if they did sin, they had to offer up sacrifices for repentance because they were never forgiven for their sins. When you initially want to be saved because you have understood that your way of life was wrong and that you are a sinner, now that's another avenue to take.

Joshua Prayed to God When Israel Was in Sin

God doesn't hear us when we sin.

And Joshua said, "Alas, O LORD God, wherefore hast thou at all brought this people over Jordan, to deliver us into the hand of the Amorites, to destroy us? Would to God we had been content, and dwelt on the other side Jordan! O Lord, what shall I say, when Israel turneth their backs before their enemies! For the Canaanites and all the inhabitants of the land shall hear of it, and shall environ us round, and cut off our name from the earth: and what wilt thou do unto thy great name?"

And the LORD said unto Joshua, "Get thee up; wherefore liest thou thus upon thy face? [God tells Joshua, "Don't pray to me while in sin."] Israel hath sinned, and they have also transgressed my covenant which I commanded them: for they have even taken of the accursed thing, and have also stolen, and dissembled also, and they have put it even among their own stuff. Therefore the children of Israel could not stand before their enemies, but turned their backs before their enemies, because they were accursed: neither will I be with you any more, except ye destroy the accursed from among you." (Joshua 7:7–12)

Israel couldn't win any wars because they were in sin.

Then they reviled him, and said, "Thou art his disciple; but we are Moses' disciples. We know that God spake unto Moses: as for this fellow, we know not from whence he is." [They are talking about Jesus after he had healed a blind man.]

The man [who had been healed] answered and said unto them, "Why herein is a marvellous thing, that ye know not from whence he is, and yet he hath opened mine eyes." (John 9:28–30)

What does the formerly blind man go on to say?

Now we know that God heareth not sinners: but if any man be a worshipper of God, and doeth his will, him he heareth. [You need to put this in context of someone outside of the church trying to get in to be saved and that's where the world is.] Since the world began was it not heard that any man opened the eyes of one that was born blind. If this man were not of God, he could do nothing.

They answered and said unto him, "Thou wast altogether born in sins, and dost thou teach us? And they cast him out." (John 9:30–34)

Many televangelists and even your ministers have taught the "sinner's prayer," but God doesn't hear sinners, so what must they do to be saved? "And he said unto them, Go ye into all the world, and preach the gospel to every creature. He that believeth and is baptized shall be saved; but he that believeth not shall be damned" (Mark 16:15-16). When you believe in the words that Jesus has been speaking to you, then you have to repent of your sins and be submerged in water, becoming baptized, and then you will be a Christian. You must forsake all the other religions and their teachings.

Then once you are baptized, which washes away all of your past sins, then you can pray to God. If you sin, you have to take care of that sin with the person you've trespassed against, and that sin is no longer on your soul.

Baptism Is Compared to Circumcision

Baptism takes water, right? Well, guess what: God made plenty of it, and the world is clueless because they have boats for recreation for the water, and they go to the beach to swim, and they drink water because the body needs water. All of this great wonder was done by God for the future use of baptism.

In the beginning God created the heaven and the earth. And the earth was without form, and void; and darkness was upon the face of the deep [water]. And the Spirit of God moved upon the face of the waters …. And God called the dry land Earth; and the gathering together of the waters called the Seas: and God saw that it was good. (Genesis 1:1–2, 10)

God the great Creator planned who knows how many years in advance that water would be the salvation for humanity. Water is all around the world to be used for salvation. Oh, what a God we serve—smart, intelligent, and full of wisdom.

Remember Noah and his family because many would say that the ark saved them, but listen to how Peter described this incident: "Which sometime were disobedient, when once the longsuffering of God waited in the days of Noah, while the ark was a preparing, wherein few, that is, eight souls were saved by water" (1 Peter 3:20). The world was disobedient. Peter the apostle states that Noah and his family were "saved by water" and not the ark. Why? The water saved Noah from the destruction of the world due to its "corruption," and it picked up the ark above the sins of man and "washed" the world clean again.

No Sinner's Prayers

When you are trying to pray to God and you acknowledge that you are a sinner and have confessed to God what He already knows, He's simply saying "Believe in these teachings and go 'get wet'; then I will hear you."

Jesus, before He began His ministry, had to be baptized because it was His father's commandment to do so, knowing that the Lord had not sinned. So, He set the stage, being the example to show the world what you must do first before coming to God. Let's read.

John "the Baptist"

John the Baptist was not of the Baptist religion; he got that name because he simply baptized believers of this new ministry, waiting on the coming of the Savior.

John was very unorthodox; he lived primitively, having very little concern for worldly views. John was the cousin of Jesus, and John would be the "forerunner" for Jesus, meaning that John would have believers ready for Christ when He came on the scene so that the Lord would have an audience of believers ready to go and help with his ministry.

In those days came John the Baptist, preaching in the wilderness of Judaea, and saying, "Repent ye: for the kingdom of heaven is at hand. For this is he that was spoken of by the prophet Esaias, saying, The voice of one crying in the wilderness, Prepare ye the way of the Lord, make his paths straight." And the same John had his raiment of camel's hair, and a leathern girdle about his loins; and his meat was locusts and wild honey. Then went out to him Jerusalem, and all Judaea, and all the region round about Jordan, and were baptized of him in Jordan, confessing their sins. (Matthew 3:1–6)

Jesus Is Baptized by John

Then cometh Jesus from Galilee to Jordan unto John, to be baptized of him. But John forbid him, saying, "I have need to be baptized of thee, and comest thou to me?"

And Jesus answering said unto him, "Suffer it to be so now: for thus it becometh us to fulfil all righteousness." Then he suffered him.

And Jesus, when he was baptized, went up straightway out of the water: and, lo, the heavens were opened unto him, and he saw the Spirit of God descending like a dove, and lighting upon him: and lo a voice from heaven, saying, "This is my beloved Son, in whom I am well pleased." (Matthew 3:13–17)

Jesus couldn't start His ministry until He was baptized. So, to be pleasing to God, you need to be baptized initially to start your Christian walk, not say a prepared "sinner's prayer."

From that time Jesus began to preach, and to say, "Repent: for the kingdom of heaven is at hand."

And Jesus, walking by the sea of Galilee, saw two brethren, Simon called Peter, and Andrew his brother, casting a net into the sea: for they were fishers. And he saith unto them, "Follow me, and I will make you fishers of men." (Matthew 4:17-19)

No "sinner's prayer" ever mentioned.

No Deathbed Confessions

Let me try to understand this concept. You're telling me that you will do all your dirt and sinning and then try to ease your way into heaven by a deathbed confession while the rest of us are fighting sins every day? God isn't that dumb.

When Jesus walked upon the face of the earth, He did things that He would never do again because the key word is walked upon the earth.

And the scribes and the Pharisees began to reason, saying, "Who is this which speaketh blasphemies? Who can forgive sins, but God alone?"

But when Jesus perceived their thoughts, he answering said unto them, "What reason ye in your hearts? Whether is easier, to say, Thy sins be forgiven thee; or to say, Rise up and walk? But that ye may know that the Son of man hath power upon earth to forgive sins, (he said unto the sick of the palsy,) I say unto thee, Arise, and take up thy couch, and go into thine house." (Luke 5:21–24)

The Thief on the Cross

But the other answering rebuked him, saying, "Dost not thou fear God, seeing thou art in the same condemnation? And we indeed justly; for we receive the due reward of our deeds: but this man hath done nothing amiss."

And he said unto Jesus, "Lord, remember me when thou comest into thy kingdom." And Jesus said unto him, "Verily I say unto thee, To day shalt thou be with me in paradise." (Luke 23:40–43)

Yes, when Jesus walked upon the earth, He forgave men their sins, but Jesus is now in heaven, and the way to be forgiven is through belief in these teachings and then to be baptized, and the Lord will add you to His church.

This Is What You Must Do to Be Saved Now

"And Jesus came and spake unto them, saying, All power is given unto me in heaven and in earth. Go ye therefore, and teach all nations, baptizing them in the name of the father, and of the Son, and of the Holy Ghost" (Matthew 28:18–19).

Acts of the Apostles

I truly believe that this book is called Acts because Rome and Greece believed in the theater—you know, "acting." So, the apostles acted out what Jesus commanded them to do, and that was to teach that Jesus is the Savior and was crucified by Rome and has risen to heaven and that man should repent and be baptized in His name to save his soul. First you must hear the teachings, believe in the teachings, be baptized, and walk in newness of life.

"What Must I Do to Be Saved?"

Men and brethren, let me freely speak unto you of the patriarch David, that he is both dead and buried, and his sepulchre is with us unto this day. Therefore, being a prophet, and knowing that God had sworn with an oath to him, that of the fruit of his loins, according to the flesh, he would raise up Christ to sit on his throne; he seeing this before spake of the resurrection of Christ, that his soul was not left in hell, neither his flesh did see corruption. This Jesus hath God raised up, whereof we all are witnesses. Therefore, being by the right hand of God exalted, and having received of the father the promise of the Holy Ghost, he hath shed forth this, which ye now see and hear. For David is not ascended into the heavens: but he saith himself, The Lord said unto my Lord, "Sit thou on my right hand, until I make thy foes thy footstool." Therefore, let all the house of Israel know assuredly, that God hath made that same Jesus, whom ye have crucified, both Lord and Christ.

Now when they heard this, they were pricked in their heart, and said unto Peter and to the rest of the apostles, "Men and brethren, what shall we do?" [Peter had convinced about three thousand Jews that this man Jesus was the Son of God who was to come and that the Jews had crucified Him and that the way of salvation came through Jesus by faith, repentance, and then baptism.] Then Peter said unto them, "Repent, and be baptized every one of you in the name of Jesus Christ for the remission of sins, and ye shall receive the gift of the Holy Ghost." (Acts 2:29–38)

Nothing is said here about praying the "sinner's prayer." Three thousand Jews were saved by believing in baptism. "And with many other words did he testify and exhort, saying, Save yourselves from this untoward generation. Then they that gladly received his word were baptized: and the same day there were added unto them about three thousand souls" (Acts 2:40–41).

At this time Peter could have said, "Pray the sinner's prayer," but that wasn't the teachings for the initial first part to become part of the church. Those that repented were baptized in Jesus's name because everything is in the name of Christ.

Remember, in Geneses 17, that under the Old Testament, to be in the "covenant relationship," you had to be circumcised, right? Now under the New Testament, you must have faith in the "spiritual circumcision" called baptism, so let's see how this works.

In whom also ye are circumcised with the circumcision made without hands, in putting off the body of the sins of the flesh by the circumcision of Christ. (Colossians 2:11)

No sprinkling or pouring water for baptism as do the Catholics and the Methodists.

[Ye are] buried with him in baptism, wherein also ye are risen with him through the faith of the operation of God, who hath raised him from the dead. (Colossians 2:12)

We Christians are submerged in water by being "buried with him," like being covered up in dirt while in the grave; this is all "similitude." When being baptized, you will be asked if you "believe" or "have faith" in Jesus Christ and His teachings, and you must confess to that truth. Then you are laid in the water, as if in death and as Jesus was laid to rest, being completely submerged in water like in a tomb or under six feet of dirt. Then you are raised up out of the water as Jesus was raised from the grave, and all of your past sins are washed away. And as Jesus had a new body, you will have one too. It's all similitude, comparisons.

When we are being baptized, God is spiritually circumcising us by cutting away our sins in the waters of baptism, like Abraham was cutting away the infectious skin during the physical circumcision. Awesome!

And you, being dead in your sins and the uncircumcision of your flesh, hath he quickened together with him, having forgiven you all trespasses; blotting out the handwriting of ordinances that was against us, which was contrary to us, and took it out of the way, nailing it to his cross. (Colossians 2:13–14)

No more Old Testament teachings. You must believe in this operation of baptism to be saved.

Buried with Christ in Baptism

Know ye not, that so many of us as were baptized into Jesus Christ were baptized into his death? Therefore, we are buried with him by baptism into death: that like as Christ was raised up from the dead by the glory of the father, even so we also should walk in newness of life.

For if we have been planted together in the likeness of his death, we shall be also in the likeness of his resurrection: knowing this, that our old man is crucified with him, that the body of sin might be destroyed, that henceforth we should not serve sin. For he that is dead is freed from sin. (Romans 6:3-7)

"Repent"

"The sacrifices of God are a broken spirit: a broken and a contrite heart, O God, thou wilt not despise" (Psalm 51:17). In Acts 2:38 it states that they were "pricked" in their heart, so you have to come to grips or terms that you have sinned against God's law and have disobeyed His Word.

Acknowledge

"Only acknowledge thine iniquity, that thou hast transgressed against the LORD thy God, and hast scattered thy ways to the strangers under every green tree, and ye have not obeyed my voice, saith the LORD" (Jeremiah 3:13).

Follow the Savior

Then cometh Jesus from Galilee to Jordan unto John, to be baptized of him. But John forbad him, saying, "I have to be baptized of thee, and comest thou to me? And Jesus answering said unto him, "Suffer it to be so now: for thus it becometh us to fulfil all righteousness." Then he suffered him.

And Jesus, when he was baptized, went up straightway out of the water: and, lo, the heavens were opened unto him, and he saw the Spirit of God descending like a dove, and lighting upon him:

And lo a voice from heaven, saying, "This is my beloved Son, in whom I am well pleased." (Matthew 3:13–17)

No Sinner's Prayer, Ever

What Are Sins?

"Whosoever committeth sin transgresseth also the law: for sin is the transgression of the law" (1 John 3:4). Sin is when we disobey the commandments of God instead of "rightly dividing the Word of Truth.".

Sins

Now the works of the flesh are manifest, which are these; Adultery, fornication, uncleanness, lasciviousness, idolatry, witchcraft, hatred, variance, emulations, wrath, strife, seditions, heresies, envyings, murders, drunkenness, revellings, and such like: of the which I tell you before, as I have also told you in time past, that they which do such things shall not inherit the kingdom of God. (Galatians 5:19–21)

Acts Shows All Baptisms

I know you have read about Saul, who became Paul, and his journey. Paul was a Pharisee, a Jew who believed in the resurrection and devout in the Law of Moses and the Ten Commandments. Paul came on the scene about AD 50 and was a devout Jew, still under the Old Law. This meant that if anyone came teaching something else against the Law of Moses, they were considered false teachers, and they were to be killed.

Paul ignorantly had Christians put into prison and even had them killed. He had to meet the Savior for himself on the road to Damascus.

Paul's Conversion

"Saul Gave His Voice Against Stephen"

And Saul was consenting unto his death. And at that time there was a great persecution against the church which was at Jerusalem; and they were all scattered abroad throughout the regions of Judaea and Samaria, except the apostles. And devout men carried Stephen to his burial and made great lamentation over him. As for Saul, he made havock of the church, entering into every house, and haling men and women committed them to prison. (Acts 8:1–3)

And Saul, yet breathing out threatening and slaughter against the disciples of the Lord, went unto the high priest, and desired of him letters to Damascus to the synagogues, that if he found any of this way, whether they were men or women, he might bring them bound unto Jerusalem. And as he journeyed, he came near Damascus: and suddenly there shined round about him a light from heaven: and he fell to the earth, and heard a voice saying unto him, "Saul, Saul, why persecutest thou me?"

And he said, "Who art thou, Lord?"

And the Lord said, "I am Jesus whom thou persecutest: it is hard for thee to kick against the pricks." [Saul recognizes that this spiritual being is someone great because he calls him Lord.]

And he trembling and astonished said, "Lord, what wilt thou have me to do?"

And the Lord said unto him, "Arise, and go into the city, and it shall be told thee what thou must do." [Salvation— how?]

And the men which journeyed with him stood speechless, hearing a voice, but seeing no man. And Saul arose from the earth; and when his eyes were opened, he saw no man: but they led him by the hand, and brought him into Damascus. (Acts 9:1–8)

Saul's Conversion

And Saul arose from the earth; and when his eyes were opened, he saw no man: but they led him by the hand, and brought him into Damascus. And he was three days without sight, and neither did eat nor drink.

And there was a certain disciple at Damascus, named Ananias; and to him said the Lord in a vision, "Ananias."

And he said, "Behold, I am here, Lord."

And the Lord said unto him, "Arise, and go into the street which is called Straight, and enquire in the house of Judas for one called Saul, of Tarsus: for, behold, he prayeth [if Saul wasn't a chosen vessel he would still be there praying until this day for two thousand years. Saul was a sinner, and he had Christians put to death so the Lord wasn't hearing his prayers until—see verse 18.], and hath seen in a vision a man named Ananias coming in, and putting his hand on him, that he might receive his sight."

Then Ananias answered, "Lord, I have heard by many of this man, how much evil he hath done to thy saints at Jerusalem: and here he hath authority from the chief priests to bind all that call on thy name."

But the Lord said unto him, "Go thy way: for he is a chosen vessel unto me, to bear my name before the Gentiles, and kings, and the children of Israel: for I will shew him how great things he must suffer for my name's sake."

And Ananias went his way, and entered into the house; and putting his hands on him said, "Brother Saul, the Lord, even Jesus, that appeared unto thee in the way as thou camest, hath sent me, that thou mightest receive thy sight, and be filled with the Holy Ghost." And immediately there fell from his eyes as it had been scales: and he received sight forthwith, and arose, and was baptized. (Acts 9:8–18)

Paul gives his account of his conversion in Acts 22. Let's read:

"Awesome," a Must Read

Men, brethren, and fathers, hear ye my defense which I make now unto you.

(And when they heard that he spake in the Hebrew tongue to them, they kept the more silence: and he saith,)

I am verily a man which am a Jew, born in Tarsus, a city in Cilicia, yet brought up in this city at the feet of Gamaliel, and taught according to the perfect manner of the law of the fathers, and was zealous toward God, as ye all are this day. And I persecuted this way unto the death, binding and delivering into prisons both men and women. As also the high priest doth bear me witness, and all the estate of the elders: from whom also I received letters unto the brethren, and went to Damascus, to bring them which were there bound unto Jerusalem, for to be punished.

And it came to pass, that, as I made my journey, and was come nigh unto Damascus about noon, suddenly there shone from heaven a great light round about me. And I fell unto the ground, and heard a voice saying unto me, "Saul, Saul, why persecutest thou me?"

And I answered, "Who art thou, Lord?"

And he said unto me, "I am Jesus of Nazareth, whom thou persecutest." And they that were with me saw indeed the light, and were afraid; but they heard not the voice of him that spake to me. And I said, "What shall I do, Lord?"

And the Lord said unto me, "Arise, and go into Damascus; and there it shall be told thee of all things which are appointed for thee to do." And when I could not see for the glory of that light, being led by the hand of them that were with me, I came into Damascus.

And one Ananias, a devout man according to the law, having a good report of all the Jews which dwelt there, came unto me, and stood, and said unto me, "Brother Saul, receive thy sight." And the same hour I looked up upon him.

And he said, "The God of our fathers hath chosen thee, that thou shouldest know his will, and see that Just One, and shouldest hear the voice of his mouth. For thou shalt be his witness unto all men of what thou hast seen and heard. And now why tarriest thou? Arise, and be baptized, and wash away thy sins, calling on the name of the Lord." (Acts 22:1–16)

Paul couldn't ask the Lord for anything until he was baptized; then he could "call on the name of the Lord."

No Sinner's Prayer or Deathbed Confessions

"Be ye followers of me, even as I also am of Christ" (1 Corinthians 11:1). "For I speak to you Gentiles, in as much as I am the apostle of the Gentiles, I magnify mine office" (Romans 11:13). I must follow the apostle Paul's example to be baptized, not the "sinner's prayer" because I'm a Gentile, and I want to get to heaven.

After Baptism

Now, how do you keep your soul free from sin? Every time you think wrong in your mind, say something wrong, or do something wrong, you take care of that sin by confessing to the one that you have wronged and then go to God in prayer, and by faith you are forgiven. "Wherefore, my beloved, as ye have always obeyed, not as in my presence only, but now much more in my absence, work out your own salvation with fear and trembling" (Philippians 2:12).

This Is How the Congregation Deals with Sin

Moreover, if thy brother shall trespass against thee, go and tell him his fault between thee and him alone: if he shall hear thee, thou hast gained thy brother. [Nothing else to say or do.] But if he will not hear thee, then take with thee one or two more, that in the mouth of two or three witnesses every word may be established. And if he shall neglect to hear them, tell it unto the church: but if he neglect to hear the church, let him be unto thee as an heathen man and a publican. (Matthew 18:15–17)

Excommunicate and have no fellowship with them until they repent before the church.

"Brethren, if a man be overtaken in a fault, ye which are spiritual, restore such a one in the spirit of meekness; considering thyself, lest thou also be tempted" (Galatians 6:1). This is the responsibility of pastors and leaders.

If I commit sins that the community knows about, I have to take care of that. No confessionals to a Catholic priest or pope. No man can forgive you of sins like trying to be like God.

The Antichrist

Antichrist, meaning not like Jesus, is a figure who will pretend to be like Jesus to deceive man. Anti is like being a spy, because this one is not true but a fake. When you pray to Mary, that's anti, because Mary isn't in the "chain of command" for prayers. Jesus said, "And whatsoever ye shall ask in my name, that will I do, that the father may be glorified in the Son." (John 14:13)

And this is the record, that God hath given to us eternal life, and this life is in his Son. [Eternal Life is not through Mary.] He that hath the Son hath life; and he that hath not the Son of God hath not life.

These things have I written unto you that believe on the name of the Son of God; that ye may know that ye have eternal life, and that ye may believe on the name of the Son of God. (1 John 5:11–13)

You don't pray on "Rosary beads" or say so many "Hail Marys" or pray on "Saint Christopher's medallions" or do a "cross" symbol with your hands across your chest or burn a cross in African slaves' yards. How do these things get you closer to Jesus? What scriptures show any of the apostles burning a cross in someone's yard and calling it an "act of God"?

Now, take a cross made of gold, silver, wood, or stone and hold it in front of your face between you and the heavens. Now God can't get through to you and you can't get through to God because the cross is blocking the view. This is a form of idolatry, and what scripture tells us to do this?

This world pays men and women millions of dollars publicizing how to be saved by the "sinner's prayer," and they will burst hell wide open because they believe in false teachers.

Know Them by Their Fruit

Enter ye in at the strait gate: for wide is the gate, and broad is the way, that leadeth to destruction, and many there be which go in thereat [many false teachers]: because strait is the gate, and narrow is the way, which leadeth unto life, and few there be that find it. [Remember Noah: only eight souls were saved because they obeyed.]

Beware of false prophets, which come to you in sheep's clothing, but inwardly they are ravening wolves. Ye shall know them by their fruits.

Do men gather grapes of thorns, or figs of thistles? Even so every good tree bringeth forth good fruit; but a corrupt tree bringeth forth evil fruit [greed]. A good tree cannot bring forth evil fruit, neither can a corrupt tree bring forth good fruit. Every tree that bringeth not forth good fruit is hewn down, and cast into the fire. Wherefore by their fruits ye shall know them.

Not every one that saith unto me, Lord, Lord, shall enter into the kingdom of heaven; but he that doeth the will of my father which is in heaven. Many will say to me in that day, Lord, Lord, have we not prophesied in thy name? And in thy name have cast out devils? and in thy name done many wonderful works? And then will I profess unto them, I never knew you: depart from me, ye that work iniquity.

Therefore, whosoever heareth these sayings of mine, and doeth them, I will liken him unto a wise man, which built his house upon a rock: and the rain descended, and the floods came, and the winds blew, and beat upon that house; and it fell not: for it was founded upon a rock. And every one that heareth these sayings of mine, and doeth them not, shall be likened unto a foolish man, which built his house upon the sand: and the rain descended, and the floods came, and the winds blew, and beat upon that house; and it fell: and great was the fall of it. (Matthew 7:13–27)

Day of Judgment

Work out your own salvation with fear and trembling. (Philippians 2:12)

And it is appointed unto men once to die, but after that the judgement. (Hebrews 9:27)

And they went up on the breadth of the earth, and compassed the camp of the saints about, and the beloved city: and fire came down from God out of heaven, and devoured them. And the devil that deceived them was cast into the lake of fire and brimstone, where the beast and the false prophet are, and shall be tormented day and night for ever and ever.

And I saw a great white throne, and him that sat on it, from whose face the earth and the heaven fled away; and there was found no place for them. And I saw the dead, small and great, stand before God; and the books were opened: and another book was opened, which is the book of life: and the dead were judged out of those things which were written in the books, according to their works. And the sea gave up the dead which were in it; and death and hell delivered up the dead which were in them: and they were judged every man according to their works. (Revelation 20:9–13)

Rome is good about cremation, but ye shall not escape the final judgment because God is going to put you back together to stand trial.

What if Christ had been cremated? Then He couldn't have been raised on the third day, right? Who told you to be cremated? Rome. See verse 13 again. Do you know how many people have died at sea since the beginning of time? Let's say you were blown up in a war at sea, and the sharks ate you; then a whale ate that shark. Then the whale died on the shore, and the birds ate the whale, and the birds flew to another continent and died. The Almighty God is going to put you back together to stand trial. You shall not escape the final judgment. "And death and hell were cast into the lake of fire. This is the second death" (Revelation 20:14).

The Kingdom Is Everlasting

I beheld, and the same horn made war with the saints, and prevailed against them; until the Ancient of days came, and judgment was given to the saints of the most High; and the time came that the saints possessed the kingdom.

Thus, he said, "The fourth beast shall be the fourth kingdom upon earth, which shall be diverse from all kingdoms, and shall devour the whole earth, and shall tread it down, and break it in pieces. And the ten horns out of this kingdom are ten kings that shall arise: and another shall rise after them; and he shall be diverse from the first, and he shall subdue three kings. And he shall speak great words against the most High, and shall wear out the saints of the most High, and think to change times and laws: and they shall be given into his hand until a time and times and the dividing of time."

But the judgment shall sit, and they shall take away his dominion, to consume and to destroy it unto the end. And the kingdom and dominion, and the greatness of the kingdom under the whole heaven, shall be given to the people of the saints of the most High, whose kingdom is an everlasting kingdom, and all dominions shall serve and obey him.

Hitherto is the end of the matter. As for me Daniel, my cogitations much troubled me, and my countenance changed in me: but I kept the matter in my heart. (Daniel 7:21–28)

"The Spirit and the Bride Say Come"

Blessed are they that do his commandments, that they may have right to the tree of life, and may enter in through the gates into the city. For without are dogs, and sorcerers, and whoremongers, and murderers, and idolaters, and whosoever loveth and maketh a lie.

I Jesus have sent mine angel to testify unto you these things in the churches. I am the root and the offspring of David, and the bright and morning star.

And the Spirit and the bride say, "Come. And let him that heareth say, Come. And let him that is athirst come. And whosoever will, let him take the water of life freely."

For I testify unto every man that heareth the words of the prophecy of this book, if any man shall add unto these things, God shall add unto him the plagues that are written in this book: and if any man shall take away from the words of the book of this prophecy, God shall take away his part out of the book of life, and out of the holy city, and from the things which are written in this book.

He which testifieth these things saith, "Surely I come quickly. Amen. Even so, come, Lord Jesus." (Revelation 22:14–20)

Disclaimer: I, the writer of this book, have sinned like every other man.

May the Lord bless those that who read this book about my understanding of the greatest book ever written, THE BIBLE.

Read the author's take on the Fourth Beast, the Son of Perdition and how one receives the Mark of the Beast "666" by celebrating those holidays on the calendar.

1 Corinthians 15:55 KJV

"O death, where is thy sting? O grave, where is thy victory?"

Several days before my mom's death as I was at her bed side she asked me about her oldest daughter whom she buried some months earlier "Shedrick she said Is Judy cold?" I said "no Mamma". She asked again "Is it raining on her?" I said "No Mamma." Then she nodded her head to say "Ok".

I think about this often because the cemetery is about 5 minutes from where we all lived and I pass by that way to my doctor's offices, so one day it was raining and I pulled into the cemetery to comfort them to let them know that everything is "Ok".

1Chorithians 15:57-58

57But thanks be to God, which giveth us the victory through our Lord Jesus Christ.58Therefore, my beloved brethren, be ye stedfast, unmoveable, always abounding in the work of the Lord, forasmuch as ye know that your labour is not in vain in the Lord.

ABOUT THE AUTHOR

Author Shedrick Crosby was born in Pensacola, Florida in 1958 to Julius and Mildred Floyd Crosby. He grew up with his three brothers and three sisters.

Married having four children.

Schools attended were Golden Elementary, Brownsville Middle School and Tate High School all of Pensacola Florida and Montgomery Junior High of Imperial Beach California.

Joined the Marines from 1976 to 1980.

Patent on The Tennis Watch in 2010.